LAUREN AN[illegible]TTI

Courage and Strength

First edition

ISBN: 978-0-7961-1248-4

This book was professionally typeset on Reedsy. Find out more at reedsy.com

To Ryan and Matthew, who taught us to love unconditionally and live life to the fullest.

To James, who symbolises that miracles do happen.

And to anyone facing challenges, know that there is always someone there for you.

You are braver than you believe, stronger than you seem, smarter than you think and loved more than you know.

Contents

Foreword

As a paediatrician, I realise how privileged I was to become part of a child's life and a family's as well. I was often there at the joyous arrival of a child into this world, and then, over the months and years, I had snapshots of their growth and development to childhood and beyond.

However, with some children and their families, by virtue of their personalities or problems and health issues, an emotional involvement was inevitable. To remain emotionally detached was humanly impossible.

Such was the case with the Spagnoletti family. I got to know them at Matthew's birth and was later introduced to Ryan. At that stage, the boys' medical issues were undefined and perplexing. Later, when the exact nature and complexity of it all was diagnosed as Cockayne's Syndrome, I recall thinking how grossly unfair life and the universe are to burden one couple and their children with such a devastating condition.

Through the years and their many challenges, I watched the boys grow at their own pace and delighted in their distinctive personalities. Perhaps because he was the firstborn, Ryan frequently objected when the attention shifted to his younger brother. While Matthew, with his happy-go-lucky outlook, was always glad to see you and interact.

My admiration knows no bounds regarding their parents, Paul and Lauren. I have never known a couple, faced with so many challenges, so determined to lead a full and everyday family life. They seemed undaunted by feeding gastronomies, drip stands, special diets, and a pharmacy's worth of medication. This family went on holiday, locally and abroad, attended every family celebration and joined in the spirit of Halloween and Christmas, ensuring that their boys never missed out on any opportunity to have fun and live life to the fullest.

Doing this takes a special sort of courage and determination, and I know their goals were achieved despite almost insurmountable problems and obstacles. They appeared to be undaunted by it all.

However, this book tells their story that I, and many others, did not fully appreciate at times. Their anger, their disappointment in some medical professionals, the many uncertainties, mourning the loss of a normal childhood and life for their boys and the growing realisation that their time with Ryan and Matthew was to be short. There were times when they voiced these, but so much of their journey has only been revealed in this book.

This book is about two ordinary people who, together, faced probably the most devastating event in any couple's life – the loss of a child. But, in their case, two children. And how they discovered such courage and fortitude to endure and survive it all along the way. I do not think they fully appreciate what an incredible example they are as a couple and family.

It has been humbling to be part of their journey and their story.

Dr Deon Smith

Preface

Like every story, you must start at the beginning.

This is a story about us, the Spagnoletti family.

Our book chronicles the extraordinary lives of our two sons, born with an exceptionally rare genetic syndrome that ,at the time, there was only 100 living diagnosed cases worldwide. It's a story that takes you through the lowest of lows and highest of highs, offering a glimpse into the complexities of raising severely ill children while navigating the demands of careers and relationships.

But it's not just a story of hardship.

It's a testament to the incredible strength and resilience of our family. In the face of unimaginable challenges, we discovered a reservoir of courage we never knew existed. As husband and wife, we share our journey of love, loss, and growth, revealing how we managed to weather the storm together.

Ultimately, this book is a beacon of hope for anyone grappling with seemingly insurmountable circumstances. We hope our story demonstrates there is a path forward, even in the darkest times. It's also a tribute to our third son, James, so he may better understand his brothers and their profound impact on our lives.

If you find yourself facing adversity, we invite you to read our book. We hope it will provide solace, inspiration, and the knowledge that, no matter how difficult the journey, you can emerge stronger and filled with hope on the other side.

This is the story of 2 incredible boys and their impact on our family and the world!

Acknowledgement

We are so grateful to have had so many people supporting us on our journey. To Our family and friends who dropped everything to be there any minute of any day that we needed them, we wouldn't have been able to do it all without you. To Cath Sheperd, thank you for helping us with our book at the very beginning. To Amy and friends and Jayne Hughes and family for giving us our CS family.To Our incredible medical team, Prof. Laugal, Dr. Billi, Karen Fieggan, Kath Megaw and a special mention to Deon Smith, who went above and beyond his duty. Words cannot express our gratitude to have had you as our paediatrician.

1

Chapter 1

Our Beginning

Lauren

It was in 1996 when we first met each other at a nightclub in Cape Town through a mutual friend. We clicked straight away and ended up talking for hours that night. There was a powerful connection between us; we could easily chat. Although we grew up in different family situations, we had a lovely balance of having much in common but different interests and goals.

Paul grew up with his Dad, Mom and brother Adam, and although he had an extended family, they were not very close to all of them. Paul was focusing on his career in IT and was very driven with clear plans for the workplace. Being competitive and sporty, he played touch rugby, rugby, squash, and cricket and, at one stage, dreamed of becoming a professional cricket player.

While I grew up with my Mom and sister, Shelly, my Dad remarried when I was very young. I spent my school holidays with my Dad and step-mom, Barbara. They had a son called Travis, and Barbara had three children from her previous marriage: Janet, Graydon, and Katherine. My two aunts, Linda and Marion, had helped look after my sister and me growing up as my Mom worked full time.

I studied teaching; my dream was to one day open a school, settle down, get married, and have two children.

After 8 months of dating, Paul was transferred to Johannesburg, and although we continued to have a long-distance relationship, we soon realised that commuting was not the answer. We both knew we wanted to get married, so why wait? As we were both traditional regarding marriage, we decided to get engaged first and had our wedding six months later. That was December 1997. We knew it was unusual to get married so young; we were only twenty and twenty-two at the time. Our family and friends were all shocked by our decision. When we look back at our wedding video and at the photos, the expression on the best man's face is priceless; when you look closely, you can imagine his thoughts, "What are you doing, mate? Are you crazy?" Duncan obviously didn't think Paul was too crazy; they are still best friends today.

Because Paul was in Johannesburg during our engagement, his weekends were very busy trying to confirm things. Our budget was very tight, so we tried to do as much as possible ourselves, but we did allow some extravagance. We hired a Rolls Royce with our names on the number plates to take us to the wedding. For the reception, we rented a school hall, and my family and I decorated it to the hilt, making it extra special. We had a spit braai for dinner.

We were super young, so in our minds, the focus needed to be on the occasion, the party. And a party it was. I hired a traditional white Cinderella dress, and Paul, the best men, (Paul's brother and best mate) and the ring bearer, wore tuxedos. And boy, did they look smart!

I had two bridesmaids, my sister and my best friend, and they had dresses made, which was quite stressful as my friend was living in the UK at the time, so we got her measurements and hoped for the best. We only got the dresses the night before!

After a few very stressful months, the day finally came, and I felt extremely calm. My Mom's house was a hive of activity, with people popping in all morning.

Eventually, the time came to leave, and it felt like a very long ride down the main road until I finally reached the church.

On the other hand, Paul got quite nervous for the first time. Until then, he had been very nonchalant about the whole thing, possibly because whilst I was organising everything, he was in Johannesburg, not really experiencing the stress of putting something like a wedding together. Basically, he simply had to rock up on the day.

We got married in the church where I was a member and had been christened, and the Minister was lovely. The service was sweet and short; some might argue it took me longer to get there than for the service itself. As it was December, we expected hot weather but didn't expect 40 degrees. Luckily, the church fans were going full speed. We hired a DJ and danced the night away. Eventually, our guests had to throw us off the dance floor and then ask us to leave.

After being kicked out of our own wedding, we departed for our honeymoon in our highly decorated and remodelled City Golf to begin our first night as husband and wife in the beautiful Vineyard Hotel in Claremont, Cape Town. We got to the Hotel so late and had to leave early the next day, so thinking back, a luxurious hotel was kind of a waste, but it was such a special night. The next day, we set off for the rest of our honeymoon in Tulbagh, also situated in the Western Cape and well-known for its good wine. Besides the fact that I got severely sunburned on day 1, it was a magnificent time and a great way to get our married life underway.

I was born to be a teacher and absolutely loved it. In my playschool report, my teacher commented that she thought I would be a teacher one day, and I proved her right. I always knew I wanted my own children one day, too. I come from a huge family with many cousins who are more like my siblings.

Paul and I had discussed having children before we got married, and although Paul had never been a kid-oriented person, he was also keen to have a family.

After our wedding, I said a very tearful goodbye to my family and moved to Johannesburg.

This new adventure came with such a surge of mixed emotions. On the one hand, I was so excited about starting my married life, finding and decorating our first home and, in a way, having more freedom now that I didn't live at home, but it was also very scary. I am generally a shy person, so I keep to myself, and now I was moving to a town I had barely ever visited, let alone lived in. I knew only my new husband and even him; I had never lived with him.

My support system was a two-hour flight away. I tried not to panic when I said my goodbyes. I remember how bittersweet it was those first few days; not only had we never lived together before, but I had always been around my family. A huge change for me.

We rented a flat in Sandton, which was tiny but such a wonderful place to start our life together. I can still remember eating dinner off a cardboard box the first few weeks while procuring all the necessary furniture to make the apartment ours. Fun, exciting and grounding times for both of us.

We had decided that even though I loved kids, we had plenty of time before starting our own family. So we made a conscious decision to invest the first few years of our marriage in us, which we both realised later to have been very valuable.

Johannesburg was hard on me; my teaching position did not work out, so I started aupairing for a family nearby. The days went by smoothly; they were lovely people, but I was not allowed to leave the property with the child because the family was extremely protective. This led to frustration, loneliness and eventually boredom. Due to my job not working out as planned and some unfortunate circumstances with friendships that had gone a little south, in 1999, we decided that Johannesburg wasn't for us anymore. Paul approached his company about getting a transfer back to Cape Town, which they agreed to, and I got a teaching position at a play school in Cape Town.

Paul

Johannesburg, for me, on the other hand, was a lot of fun. I made a big group of friends quickly both at work as well as on the sports field, where I played mostly cricket, a bit of rugby, some touch rugby, and hockey (of all things - mostly due to my cricket mates convincing me to fill in for a few games here and there) and action cricket a few times. My career was doing well, and I saw a great future for me in the "big smoke" — as Capetonians affectionately called Johannesburg. I realised Lauren was unhappy, so it was important not to only think of myself. Fortunately, my company recognised my value and was happy to transfer me back to Cape Town. As they say, "happy wife, happy life". I also knew and believed that whilst the Cape Town office was smaller and wasn't the hustle and bustle of the head office, that in itself would create opportunity for me. I just needed to make it happen ... so I thought, let's see where this goes!

Back to Cape Town we went; I was looking forward to reconnecting with my mates and family. We found a flat in Hout Bay, so another chapter began for us. This was great because if we were going to move from the city of money and career growth, I thought it was best we lived at the beach. The year was going well, and we were so happy to be back home. I also continued to involve myself in a lot of sports. Golf was now high on my sporting agenda. I still played cricket and touch rugby, but rugby had fallen off my plate.

Then Lauren was offered the opportunity to take over the playschool where she was teaching, which meant buying the property, too.

It was a huge thing to contemplate, considering we were so young, but what an opportunity for Lauren to have her own school and for us to get into the property market. We had thought about buying a house and loved Hout Bay, but being so young made it difficult to get the necessary finance for such an upmarket suburb in Cape Town.

All the banks declined our finance application, and we lost hope. Then, out of the blue, ABSA gave us a bond. It was a miracle. The house was not perfect, but it had a bar and a really cool built-in braai with a gazebo, which was good enough for me. We were ecstatic.

Life continued, Lauren's business went well, and my career flourished.

When I was 20, I had defined certain goals for my business career, including being in Sales Management by 35, National Sales Management by 38 and a Company Director by 40 (at a high level). Career-wise, I became a national sales manager by 30 and a director by 35. Now, I have been fortunate to hold a number of executive positions in various IT companies, from start-ups to SMEs and corporate organisations alike.

As a child, I remember my Dad and I used to go to the dunes and ride his beach buggy. En route, we drove down a road covered in trees. I had dreamt of living there, not knowing where "there" was … turn the page forward, and our first house is not more than 250 meters from that road, and it turns out that street and dunes were in Hout Bay. Visualisation is a powerful tool!

From 2000 to 2002, everything floated along, and we were happy and settled with our lives, so we decided it was time for our next chapter … kids!

2

Chapter 2

The Little Person Who Made Us Parents

Lauren

Before we started making plans to have kids, we didn't know about the possible problems and setbacks that could happen. These include problems with getting pregnant, where timing is very important, and problems that could occur during pregnancy.

I was under the impression I would get pregnant the first time trying, get fat, have a natural birth, and breastfeed for a year, and that would be the start of our parenthood – perfect! It didn't work out like that at all, and if it had, our book would be a very boring story to write!

The day my period was due, I took a urine test that came back very faint but positive.

I went straight to the doctor to double-check my test against a blood test. She confirmed I was 3 weeks pregnant. It seemed unreal. Telling family and friends was so exciting; we didn't wait until it was "safe" to tell everyone. Honestly, we never once doubted everything wouldn't be perfect or that anything bad would happen to us. Such was our naive thinking.

I put the urine stick in an envelope (when we think about it now, it wasn't the most sanitary way of telling people) and gave it to Paul's parents. I will never forget when Paul's Dad saw it; he looked quite puzzled. He's a super smart guy, but we had stumped him.

When we told him it meant he would be a grandpa, his face lit up, and he had such a huge smile on his face; he came and gave me a big, strong hug, one of the first hugs he had ever given me.

I didn't even feel pregnant until about 8 weeks when I began feeling nauseous, but nothing I couldn't manage!

We had our first scan, and the doctor referred to the baby as a shrimp; it all seemed amazing, a dream come true.

At 9 weeks, I started craving peaches, and by 11 weeks, I couldn't handle the smell of cooked chicken. I still weighed 49kgs, so I hadn't put on any weight at all.

Our 12-week scan went well, and at this stage, Paul didn't want to find out the sex, but I did, so it was very frustrating for me not knowing, as I am a planner and an organiser.

At 16 weeks, I began to feel butterflies; that's when my pregnancy really started to feel real!

Paul

When we decided it was time to try for a baby, I thought it would take a while so I would have time to get used to the idea. Little did I know it would happen in the first month of trying.

I was flabbergasted when Lauren told me she was pregnant; it all happened so fast. Was I ready?

Even when we went for the first scan, I was still somewhat in denial.

When Lauren started feeling the baby move, it was then that I thought I was aware that we were really having a baby, and this wasn't a figment of my imagination.

It had become an exciting journey for Lauren, but for me, it was all too real, and like many guys (although I'm sure only a few admit it), the feeling of entrapment was a reality. Not in a very negative way, but I was struck by the enormity of the responsibility that comes with parenthood.

In a way, I had a mini midlife crisis. Luckily, I didn't have a lot of money, so this didn't mean extravagant sports cars and the like, although that would have been nice, but more the panic that our freedom would come to an end. Something I really valued and enjoyed.

This placed pressure on our relationship, but over the next few weeks, I realised that we would still be the same people and that it didn't have to mean our carefree way of existence was ending. We worked through our individual feelings, and although we dealt with things differently, we worked it out.

Without knowing it, this test would build the foundation for us to get through the many unexpected tough situations we would face.

At 23 weeks, we went for our big scan. Lauren used her powers of persuasion, but eventually, I agreed to find out the sex of our baby. We found out it was a boy, which was no surprise, as the Spagnoletti family is mainly made up of boys. I was ecstatic! The idea of having a son was a dream come true. The thought of having a girl was quite daunting for me, so having a son I could understand and watch and enjoy sports and rough and tumble with was super exciting. I started dreaming of the future quality times ahead, which would be amazing. My parents, specifically my mother, as my dad worked long hours, were very involved in my sports as a child and watched almost all my games growing up. I looked forward to the same privilege with my son.

We were over the moon, all of us, our first baby, the first grandson. It was absolutely the most exciting few months. Seeing the thrill on my parent's faces at the prospect of their first grandson, especially my Dad, was cool. It really made me so happy that he was so excited, not that this was a surprise, just that my happiness was his happiness, which was awesome.

At 24 weeks, we sat in the movies watching the 8-Mile film, and the baby started kicking. I was able to feel him moving for the first time. I was already a huge Eminem fan; this was now amplified. It is still one of my favourite movies and brings back such special memories. I am unsure if that is because of feeling the baby kick or the actual movie. Sorry 8-Mile! Little did we know that Eminem would feature quite a bit in the first few years of your life, my son.

Lauren

At 26 weeks, our gynae confirmed the sex of our baby and noticed that my placenta was low-lying, which was what my mom had experienced when she was pregnant with me. The Doctor was not worried and believed the placenta would still move.

My tummy was really stretching by now, and I'd put on 9kgs, which was to be expected!

Being a teacher and a very organised person, I started preparing the nursery by painting and sewing bedding. I hated sewing but found that this was something I wanted to do.

We chose a seaside theme because we lived in Hout Bay, near the beach. I found material, sewed a duvet cover, bumper and pillow for the cot, and painted baby blue halfway up the walls. I stencilled lighthouses in different colours all around the room as a border.

I must have packed and repacked his clothes a million times; so great was the anticipation and excitement in our home, much like any other expectant parent, I would imagine.

Everything seemed to be going well until, at 28 weeks, I was sent to a specialist. We thought this was strange but assumed it must be routine because our gynae hadn't mentioned anything. When the specialist told us our doctor was concerned about the baby's growth, I burst out crying, and as soon as we got home, I started phoning around to change doctors.

I can recall the drive home in the car; that day seemed so long, the disbelief and the knot in my stomach. We decided to stay with our doctor in the end, as we wanted to have our boy at Kingsbury Hospital, where I was born.

I was immediately ordered to take bed rest, and at 30 weeks, our doctor told us to expect our baby early. How fast things changed; only a week ago, we were blissfully unaware of any problems and had thought everything was going perfectly.

We are naturally positive people, so we figured that early meant the baby would come at around 38 weeks. We could manage that. "Um, no," she said, "he could come next week!" We were completely thrown. We had no idea how serious this was.

In some ways, it was exciting that we didn't have to wait 9 months to see our boy, but at the back of our minds, we also knew that babies needed to stay in their mom's tummies for as long as possible.

I went for a steroid injection after that appointment with the view of coming back the next day for another shot, but in the morning, I woke up with red, itchy blotches all over my tummy and back. The doctors were not happy for me to have steroids again. Clearly, I had had an allergic reaction to the first dose. So, home we went and back to bed for me. The only outing from then on was every few days, when I had to go to the hospital to get checked and monitored.

I didn't feel much movement one day, so we went in to be monitored, but all was good. The Doc sent me home and told me to have a Coke, and the love of Coke started for our little man.

One Coke later, our little guy was doing flick-flaks!!

Luckily, being the super-duper-organised one, everything was ready for the baby; the problem was we were unprepared for a premature one.

I borrowed some prem clothes from my step-sister who had prem twins the year before. I remember looking through the clothes and thinking there was no way my baby could ever be that tiny. The little blue baby-grow was so perfect but looked like a doll's outfit.

My baby shower now had to be planned quickly as we didn't know how long I had.

One night, I got into my PJs, ready to watch a movie we had chosen. Just before we started the video, the phone rang. It was my mom (the phone was on the opposite side of the house). We were just having a regular chat, and I heard a dog barking, which my Mom said was her dog. I thought nothing of it, said goodbye and returned to the TV room, where I nearly did go into labour. The room was filled with friends and family; they had snuck in while I was on the phone with my mom, who was also sneaking in, and my dog was barking.

Talk about getting completely blindsided in your own house!

The coordination and effort in organising this baby shower must have been something else. My family are super close, so I don't know how everyone kept it secret. I was beyond spoiled; the baby had enough outfits to change three times a day, nappies galore, PJs for myself, blankets, hooded towels and toiletries enough to last a lifetime.

At 33 weeks, I went to the gynae by myself as Paul was in Johannesburg, only to be told by my doctor that she wasn't happy as the baby hadn't grown, my blood pressure was up, and there was protein in my urine.

She wanted me to have a caesarean that day .... I was distraught; I couldn't have our first baby without Paul. I asked my mom to accompany me if Paul didn't return. I was admitted straight away, put in a private room, and attached to a baby monitor, with the view that if things worsened, my son would come out immediately. I didn't see our gynae again until I was in the theatre. Thinking back, this was so wrong. I was a first-time Mom; I had been admitted nearly two months earlier than I should have been with my husband in Johannesburg. I sat attached to machines all day, not knowing what to expect when having a Caesar, let alone what to expect with a 33-week-old prem baby. We really should have had an opportunity to chat with her about questions we had and had events explained to us. I totally get it. This was just another Caesar to them, but to us, this was the start of our parenthood journey.

I phoned Paul, and he had to get the earliest flight back. Luckily, everything remained the same, so the plan was to operate the next day at lunchtime, but when Paul arrived that night, we were told they would do the procedure first thing in the morning. We didn't tell any of our family about this change.

Paul

While Lauren was having a stressful time with things back in Cape Town, I was to learn some disturbing facts about business and how cold people can be. I received an urgent call from Lauren whilst in Johannesburg at our annual strategy breakaway. The timing could not have been worse. I represented the coastal region, so it was an important part of the 3-day workshop in determining how we would grow our company that year. My career was super important to me, and I was highly ambitious. Despite that, nothing was going to stop me from being at my wife's side on the day of the birth of our first child. To say this conversation did not go down well with my boss was an understatement! In fact, he said I could not leave and instructed his PA not to arrange flights or transport to the airport for me. I was shocked by his actions. I decided that seeing my son being born was more important than my career, so I got a taxi and changed my flights with help from his PA. This was to be a career-limiting move, but I guess also an illustration of this management's true colours, so off to Cape Town I went one day into the conference. I was excited and a bundle of energy, praying like crazy that I would not miss this precious event. I rushed to the hospital excited, anxious, and nervous all at the same time. At least I was to have some breathing space as the birth had been delayed.

Lauren

The evening before the Caesar, we asked if we could see the Neonatal Unit and some of the prem babies just to get an idea of what we were in for. We saw some really small babies, but it never dawned on us that our boy would be even smaller.

We had no idea how our lives were going to change. I thought to myself, *OK, prem baby means smaller*; that's fine, as I loved small babies. So what if our boy needed to stay in the hospital a few days longer than me?

I was trying to put the whole thing in context, and even while looking at these tiny little babies, I still didn't get it. We were clueless. That night, we sat in the hospital room and debated names until we decided on Ryan Peter Spagnoletti for our boy.

Ryan means little king, and Peter is after Paul's dad (a bit of a tradition within the Spagnoletti family). Peter also had special meaning to me as my uncle, Peter, whom I was close to, had passed away a few years before. When morning came, I was unbelievably calm. I bathed, and the nurse checked I had shaved properly. I hadn't, and dry shaving is not pleasant ... then I walked to the theatre; ignorance was bliss!

The Caesar went well, and Ryan came out screaming! The doctor held him up, all swaddled in a towel. I remember thinking, there's no way that's my boy; that's way too small, but it was him, the tiniest little face I had ever seen.

Ryan Peter Spagnoletti was born on Friday the 13th of June 2003 at 9 am and weighed 1,6 kg.

I didn't get the opportunity to hold him as he started having problems breathing, so they took him to the neonatal unit. Paul went with them while they stitched me up, and I remember feeling so happy; I couldn't believe I was finally a mom. My dream had come true!

Paul

It was just such an amazing experience to watch my son being born. Watching the Caesar was a miracle of modern medicine. To see the surgeon cutting open your wife's stomach, not for what it is but rather for the wonderful result. The event was incredible; watching them bring Ryan out screaming was possibly one of the most emotional days of my life (and there were to be many more, both happy and sad). For the first time ever, I understood the gravitas of what it meant to be a dad; the emotion was overflowing, and I had to be one of the happiest people on the planet at that moment. So much so that after I returned to the theatre, I said to Lauren, "Let's do that again!"I loved the thrill of it and even thought of offering my services to be in the theatres with other moms. I could witness births repeatedly, I thought to myself, what a truly beautiful experience it was. I was blessed to be able to witness such an amazing event of nature.

I had a son!

Lauren

Later that day, the doctor came to us to say that Ryan needed a bit more support with his breathing, so they were putting him on a ventilator. At no point were we worried about him. Thinking back now, we realise how little we knew about hospitals, medicines and hospital equipment; we knew nothing. The first day and night in the hospital was a blur, so I remembered only a few things.

I can clearly recall hearing someone in the passage asking for Lauren Stedman (my maiden name), and then my step-sister Kath walked in, wanting to wish me good luck. Little did she know that Ryan had already arrived. I can still remember her eyes filling with tears when she heard the news. Phoning everyone to tell them my son had arrived was the best part, and of course, everyone was so surprised when I called as they were still expecting me only to have him after lunch. The day after he was born, I was determined to go and see him, but as I moved to get up, I realised that having a c-section was not for sissies, and I had to be wheeled to the neonatal unit in a wheelchair.

I hadn't seen him since his birth the day before, which had been for maybe two minutes before he had been rushed to ICU. I just stared at him. This tiny little person was inside my tummy, and now he was here, so small but so perfect.

I could only touch his hand once they had smothered my hands with alcohol. He was connected to many machines that were beeping away, and he didn't like to be touched, which made me feel like a failure as all I wanted was to hold my baby boy.

Before I could dwell too much on anything, I was whisked away in my wheelchair by Nurse Cheryl at quite a speed.

"Right, let's get some milk for him." "But I don't have any," I replied. "Yes, you do," she said, squeezing my boob. Holy crap, I nearly fell out of the wheelchair. I had milk. I had always heard of your milk coming in, but I thought it took a few days before anything would happen. After Nurse Cheryl had shown me what to do, I sat there milking myself, and boy, was I chuffed.

Ryan was fitted with a nasogastric tube, which is a tube that enters through the nose. His sucking reflex hadn't developed yet, so they started feeding him a whopping 1 ml per hour via the tube.

It would be a long road, but we were still unaware of how long.

Being in the ICU meant no visitors; I only wanted to show my baby off. So the next day, when it was visiting hours, I borrowed a mirror so visitors outside could see his tiny little face in the mirror. When my Mom saw him, she said his head was as big as a peach.

The days in the hospital became more and more frustrating for me.

Every few hours, I had to express milk, and I became increasingly envious of all the moms holding and breastfeeding their new babies while my tiny Ryan didn't even like it when I touched his hand. This was not how I had planned the beginning of parenthood.

Paul

My days were spent juggling work and getting to the hospital as often as possible to be with Lauren, see my son, and get news of his progress. Like Lauren, I was not worried at this stage. Thinking back, Lauren and I were lucky this was our firstborn, and we were the first of our friends to have kids, so we had very little frame of reference. We might have been much more stressed if we had had a traditional experience. It is also very much in my nature to shrug things off and not take them too seriously until I need to. For the most part, I remained calm.

Lauren

The day came when I was discharged, and my emotions were high. I debated whether to pay and stay until Ryan was allowed out, but we had no idea how long that would be. After months of excitement and planning, my baby was here, just next door, and yet I wasn't allowed to touch or hold him.

I was still in pain from the Caesar, and my boobs were getting fuller, but I was packing my hospital bag and getting ready to leave the hospital without my precious little boy. I knew he was in the right place, but stepping out of the maternity ward was hard. I went home to an empty house and a nursery waiting for a baby.

The next three weeks kind of rolled into a blur. I couldn't drive, so I relied on lifts to and from the hospital and was still expressing every couple of hours and putting it into brown bottles with a sticker to indicate the date. We would race up to the neonatal unit daily (Paul had a slight advantage, with me just having had major abdominal surgery) to see how Ryan was doing. We would check how much oxygen he was getting through the ventilator and how much weight he had put on. Some days, we felt like we were making progress, and others seemed like we went backwards. Finally, after a week, he came off the ventilator, and the big day arrived! We were allowed to hold him.

Oh my god, how tiny was our baby, how precious, how perfect. The most perfect, beautiful boy we had ever seen.

I can still remember looking at his body and thinking that every element, even though they were small, was just so perfect: 10 fingers, 10 toes.

I remember Nurse Cheryl saying they hadn't had a 33-weeker who was that sick in a long time, and even then. I didn't realise how sick our boy was nor what a fighter he had become!

From then on, I spent the whole day in the neonatal unit. I was allowed to practice kanga care; some days, his statistics went crazy, and I felt my boy didn't love me, but with time, Ryan got used to being handled, and kanga care became easier. I was even allowed to give him 1 ml per hour via his nasogastric tube. Finally, some progress! Even though I spent so much time at the hospital and the staff were amazing, it just wasn't the same as having my baby at home. Every morning, I would ask permission just to come into the neonatal unit, and then once settled, I would simply do my thing. We got to know all the staff, but Nurse Cheryl was our favourite. We chatted with her a lot, and she gave us some lovely advice, which we used for all three of our boys.

-Take lots of photos. I haven't stopped since that day!

-And remember, babies come into your world, not the other way around, so keep living and vacuuming.

We still have contact with Cheryl and will always be grateful for having her with us during Ryan's stay in the hospital.

Even though he was off the ventilator, it didn't mean Ryan was out of the woods. He spent a week on oxygen and then another week in the incubator.

We gave him a dummy to try and encourage his sucking reflex, but the dummy nearly covered his nose. It was so big in comparison to his tiny face. I had been sleeping with a little stuffed dog, so it had my smell on it, and I placed that in the incubator. Paul bought a mini rugby ball for the incubator; the indoctrination process started early!

I remember on my birthday, which was two weeks after Ryan was born, arriving at the incubator, and stuck on the outside was a round mint chocolate with a paper smiley face. It said 'Happy Birthday, Mommy'. The nurses had placed it there. I still have that smiley face today. Also, on my birthday, the grandparents were allowed to hold Ryan, a very special day for everyone. It was an especially beautiful moment when my mom got to hold Ryan for the first time. Twenty-six years to the day she had brought me into the world at the very same hospital.

After two weeks, I was allowed to breastfeed Ryan, but it didn't go very well as his sucking reflex was quite weak, so he got tired quickly. We used bottles, and I expressed milk, much to my disappointment. Luckily, the hospital had organised for me to rent a great electric pump. At two weeks, he was allowed 5 ml per hour; then, we moved to 10 ml every two hours. Progress was being made, even if it was slow, but it was what we needed to keep our spirits up. From day one, we learnt to appreciate the small steps, something we would have to remember over the next few years.

The three weeks Ryan was in the hospital were such a surreal time. We fished to try to get answers as to when they thought he could go home, but we didn't get much response. The general rule, we were told, was that he had to weigh at least 2 kgs and drink well. We learnt to acknowledge and rejoice in the little things; every gram he put on was a day closer to taking him with us, and when we got there, and he had lost a gram, boy, were we disappointed. There were times we didn't think we were ever going to take him home. Then, out of the blue, our Pediatric Doctor said he thought Ryan could go home that week. We were beyond excited but didn't want to get our hopes up or anyone else's, so we didn't tell anyone what the doctor had said. We had decided when we found out it was going to be a boy that we wanted him circumcised, so the agreement was he would be circumcised in the hospital, and if he was drinking well after that, we could take our boy home.

The circumcision went well, and we stayed another night to ensure he was good. So on 5 July 2003, after 3 weeks in hospital, we were discharged with Ryan weighing 1,8kgs.

Paul came to fetch us, and we very carefully put our precious boy in the car seat, which was huge for him. I sat in the back with the biggest smile on my face while Paul drove home, the slowest he had ever driven.

Paul

I don't think I had ever seen Lauren with a bigger smile or happier in my life. It was infectious; I was over the moon myself. That drive home, I must have checked my rear-view mirror every second to ensure Lauren and Ryan were okay. I phoned the grandparents on the way to ask them what time they were coming to the hospital and to say we wouldn't be there. They were all so excited, and of course, they rushed over to our house.

Our home was super busy the next few days, and Lauren's Dad came down to see him, too; he had decided to wait until Ryan was out of the hospital.

3

Chapter 3

Tests, Hospitals and Shattered Dreams

Paul

At two months, I noticed a little bulge in Ryan's groin area, which we checked out, and it turned out to be inguinal hernias. Luckily, we knew the doctor as he had just circumcised Ryan, so back to the hospital, we went to have them repaired. Besides that, Ryan's first six months were awesome. We were taking Parenthood in our stride and loving it! We took loads of photos, and Ryan got christened in January. Lauren had chosen an old-fashioned christening outfit. It was white with pale blue around the collar and some white and pale blue little shoes. He was christened in the church we got married in, and we had asked my best mate Duncan and his wife Amy to be Ryan's godparents. It was a very special day for a very special boy. Lauren's Dad and Barbara had come down, but after the service, they told us that Lauren's Gran had passed away that morning, so they had to leave immediately.

Lauren was so upset; she was very close to her gran, so, unfortunately, the day was a very bittersweet one.

Like every parent, we had so many hopes and dreams for our family, especially for Ryan.

Ryan grew nicely but slowly, and some of his milestones were a bit delayed, but we put that down to him being prem. He was such a happy, friendly little guy, and that was all that mattered to us!

At his six-month check-up, our new paed (we had changed doctors because ours was just too busy) suggested we have an MRI scan. He wanted to check Ryan's head size, so we booked it. I was uncomfortable with hospitals to start with, and second to that, we had been sent to a private hospital I didn't like. I was uneasy. They had to sedate him twice as they took so long to come and get him. It was a nightmare day, and we still won't go back to that hospital if given a choice. Can you imagine a 6-month-old child whom they sedate and then almost forget about and must sedate a second time? I was beside myself and didn't need much of an excuse to dislike that hospital further.

We saw the doctor afterwards; he thought we should see a neurologist. When we asked why, he just said he was concerned about his growth, but it wasn't urgent. We knew our baby was just fine, but Lauren made an appointment for 3 months later anyway, and then I forgot about it and carried on with my daily life. The day we were supposed to go to the neurologist, they phoned to cancel as something had come up. Lauren burst out crying, not realising how anxious she had been until then.

We finally got to see the doctor in March 2004. She examined Ryan and seemed happy with him. We said our goodbyes, but as we got to the door, she said, "Your son reminds me of someone with cerebral palsy (C.P.)." We got into the lift and looked at each other. I looked straight at Lauren, "Did she just say our son looks like someone with cerebral palsy?" We were completely stunned. We weren't even one hundred per cent sure what C.P. was, but we knew it had a negative connotation.

Lauren went straight to her mom, distraught, and together, they Googled C.P., trying not to panic at the same time. I went back to work and put it to the back of my mind. I chose to focus on the positives, which were, at this point, that we probably misheard her. My beautiful son Ryan was the happiest, cutest little boy ever, and everything would be fine. I always had the ability to remain very calm when the pressure mounted and for downplaying negative things. I would rather choose to find and focus on the positive. This would become a great source of strength for us as a family. Lauren, on the other hand, was very organised and had an innate ability to research things and get to the bottom of a situation so that we as a family knew how to deal with it, so actually, OUR abilities complemented each other.

When Lauren got home, she wrote to the doctor, who referred us to the paediatric neurologist, saying what had been implied and that he had given us false hope. We were so upset he hadn't mentioned any of his concerns. As soon as he received the letter he phoned Lauren and was very apologetic but we never went back to him again.

The new neurologist now wanted to send Ryan for what she said were tests for C.P., so we went to the lab, and while we were waiting to go in, Lauren looked at the letter. It said they were going to be testing for Angelman Syndrome. Lauren was so confused as no one had mentioned this to us, and she immediately Googled it. The results nearly caused us both to have a heart attack. Lauren phoned the neurologist in a fury, and all she said was, "You can't test for C.P." The bedside manner, or lack thereof, was just earth-shattering; she had the E.Q. and compassion of a lifeless anthill!

Since that day, Lauren has opened and scrutinised all doctors' letters!

Lauren

The tests for Angelman Syndrome came back negative, and we cannot tell you the relief we felt. We kind of "forgot" about the testing for a while and tried to focus on our boy. I totally understand the neurologist has a terrible job; she sees children who don't fit in the box and often has to break bad news to parents, but it doesn't mean you suggest things when parents are leaving the rooms or lie to them about what you are testing for. She really could have been more empathetic. We never went back to that doctor again. We had begun the journey of finding out who the good and bad guys in the medical profession of Cape Town were. So far, our doctor and neurologist were of the former!

Despite the horrible experience with the doctor and many unanswered questions, we organised a big first birthday for our boy. Birthdays are a huge deal for me, so we planned a lovely party for Ryan.

He looked super smart in his jeans, a red striped top and red takkies. Paul's Dad made him a motorbike birthday cake, and he was unbelievably spoiled! His room looked like a toy store, from teddy bears to ride-on vehicles to clothes. This boy was so loved!

In August 2004, we went to see another neurologist as Ryan wasn't crawling yet, and they diagnosed Ryan with "C.P.". C.P., otherwise known as cerebral palsy, is an injury or abnormal development of the brain which can occur before, during or immediately after birth. It is very hard to find out exactly when the injury occurred, so we had a lawyer request my medical records, but after looking at them, there were no conclusive findings.

Paul

In September 2004, we went to the Red Cross hospital, one of the top children's hospitals in South Africa, for a milk scan as Ryan was having problems with feeding and vomiting. The scan didn't go well and showed Ryan had severe reflux. We were then referred to another doctor at another hospital who, in October 2004, recommended and performed a Nissen Fundoplication (essentially tying of the stomach to reduce the ability to vomit) and placed a peg, which is a feeding tube, straight into his tummy. This would enable us to feed him without him having to take food physically via his mouth. This was quite a thing!

They would only allow one parent to go in with him, so we decided that while we would go to the hospital, Lauren would go into the theatre room with Ryan. She would then sit with him until he was sedated and come out once he was asleep. For what seemed like an eternity, it ended up as close to two hours of surgery. Eventually, we were told the surgery was done, and we could go and see our boy. On the way back, Lauren quickly went to the loo. It couldn't have been more than a few minutes, but by the time Lauren made it down, I was being escorted out of the recovery room in a complete state of panic and grief. I had walked into the recovery room (God knows how I managed to get into the recovery room unescorted) to find Ryan screaming like he was possessed and 3 nurses sitting on top of him, trying to calm him down. This was too much for me. I went wild - pushing the nurses and doctors to the side to rescue my traumatised son. I was overpowered and manhandled from the room and taken back to the waiting room where Lauren was waiting I was very surprised to see myself being escorted out.

Once Ryan had settled, he was taken back to the paed ward, where he spent ten days in the hospital; it was major surgery for such a little boy.

In the beginning, it was trial and error to see how much food Ryan could tolerate. We struggled with the whole idea of syringing milk into his tummy. It was completely unnatural, but we also knew our boy had to eat. I can remember the first feed as being very scary because Ryan would be up and awake, and I would syringe some milk into his tummy, and he would instantly fall asleep; it was crazy! We were eventually allowed home, and it took some getting used to, but this peg thing was such a blessing. No fighting with food, and we could put medicine in it. It was actually brilliant, every child should have one, we joked!☺

Lauren

2005 was basically a blur of doctor's appointments, waiting rooms and hospitals. We tried everything that was suggested to us, and I mean everything. For every little concern or symptom, I would Google until I had answers.

I flew to Johannesburg for a week to do a course on cranial sacral therapy. Paul's uncle John very kindly paid for me to do the course, as we didn't have the money. This alternative therapy uses gentle touch to palpate the synarthrodial joints of the cranium and light touch to the patient's spine and pelvic bones.

I'm unsure if this helped, but the week after doing the course, Ryan said a few more words. When I think back about that week in Joburg, I cannot help but smile. Ryan and I stayed with John and Sylvia (Paul's aunt and uncle) and their boys Craig and Brad, and one afternoon, I asked Sylvia, who is a hairdresser, to cut and highlight my hair. While I was having that done, Craig and Brad were looking after Ryan. About two hours later, I got back, and there was Ryan sitting on the boys' lap, watching T.V. and finishing off a tub of chocolate mousse. Half the dessert was all over his cheeks and mouth, and there on his tiny face, the biggest smile ever.

Needless to say, we had a terrible night's sleep, and Ryan made about a hundred poos the next day. I think his tummy was in shock from actually getting food, but what a wonderful memory!

Paul

John (whom we affectionately called Joss) and I were very close and had somehow always been, even though growing up, my mother and her brothers lived in different Provinces. During our time in Joburg, we had gotten much closer to Joss and Sylvia, and they became more than family; they became our best friends. I think primarily through this time, the bond between us, especially Lauren and Sylvia, went to a new level. Joss and Sylvia really opened up their hearts, minds, home, and family to us and were incredibly supportive.

Lauren

We also started *Time Together,* a moms and babes programme run in Hout Bay. I met Karen, who ran it, and she was so lovely! I was so excited about sharing this with Ryan and thought it would be a great way to meet moms with children the same age. Well, let's say it did not turn out how I envisioned it.

Don't get me wrong, Karen was excellent, and we are still friends today, but personally, I found it very emotionally challenging.

You don't mean to compare children, but when everyone else's child is streaks ahead, it is hard not to get upset. So, instead of making new friends, I kept to myself and didn't talk much.

I used to get so cross with the moms complaining that their child slept too much or ate too much; I just wanted to scream at them and slap them on the head. After nearly every session, I would come home, have a cigarette (my new habit since life threw me daily challenges) and cry. Paul told me to remember everything is relative, but eventually, for my sanity, I had to give it up.

Paul

Having a child who didn't fit in the box taught us about the value of life and the privileges we had by being "normal". They added great perspective to our lives. One of the most significant teachings I gained was an insight into relativity. Through my discussions with Lauren and her challenges with Time Together, I realised that whilst this was extremely hard for Lauren, others had it even harder. I remember Lauren being particularly irritated as a child bumped its head whilst crawling, and the mother reacted as if her child had been shot or something. Lauren was upset as she would have given anything just for Ryan to be able to crawl.

The reality was we needed to be grateful that at least Ryan could bum-shuffle. Many parents had to deal with children who were born as paraplegics, and some people couldn't even have children. This realisation has shaped much of how I have learnt to react to situations in life; what a blessing from our precious children, a great gift. A practical example of this is everyday traffic, something we all have to deal with and is equally frustrating, especially the person who pulls in front of you when you have been patiently waiting at an off-ramp. Most people go crazy, throwing every sign and voicing every profanity they can think of at the transgressive, but realise this: whilst you are going crazy in your car, do they even notice? This happened to me one day. I got so cross and cursed the individual, as most do. At the end of a very trying day, I got home in a bad mood. As I reflected on my day to work out why I was in such a negative state, I realised it all started with that "idiot" who pulled in front of me. I thought about it. Did he even look in his rear-view mirror? How was his day now? In all probability, he had had a great day and got to where he was going on time. On the other hand, I had a crap day and all for something that cost me 20 seconds of my life. Something to think about, right? Now, I wave a guy in; at the end of the day, he might be in a rush for something really important, a big meeting, an interview, getting someone to a hospital, who knows. I live by this and try to apply it to all aspects of my life.

Lauren

As time went by, I found the roles in my life were changing big time. Not only was I a teacher, a mother and a wife, but now also an investigator. I became a detective in figuring out what Ryan's needs were.

Our biggest aim was to focus on Ryan's muscle tone with Botox and physio and try to sort out his ears so that we could get a proper reading. Unfortunately, because Ryan always had ear infections, we were unable to get an accurate reading because there was always fluid in the ear.

His vomiting stopped for a while but then started again, and when we chatted to the doctor about it, he blamed us for pushing feeds. We had no training for the peg or the amounts to give at one time. We were fumbling in the dark, and we felt we had no support. The peg turned out to be troublesome as we had to turn it every few hours so it didn't get stuck.

We returned to the Red Cross desperate for help, but no one had ever seen a peg. I remember feeling so isolated, so alone; if the Red Cross couldn't help us, was there anyone who could? Although Paul was very supportive and always there if I needed him, I preferred to be at all the appointments myself. Paul was working a full-time job, so it was easier for me to get to the hospital, but sometimes I felt resentment towards him. He, at least, had his work as a distraction. Family and friends didn't know how to relate and found it challenging to understand what we were going through. Everyone had advice and tried to offer an answer, but no one knew. Often, people would ask, "Have you tried giving Ryan sweets or chocolate? Every child loves that to eat!" We learnt to nod and smile as we didn't want to hurt anyone's feelings, but all I wanted to do was scream; my child doesn't want to fucking eat!!

We would try to feed Ryan, but he didn't want to take food the usual way. We had to use the syringe 90% of the time. One night, Ryan even pulled the peg out, and we had to phone the surgeon to come to our house to help us put it back in. He was very irate; we had phoned him, and he told us it was impossible to pull it out, and yet our little boy had. It just wasn't working, so we started looking for a more supportive doctor.

Thankfully, we had met a lovely GP with paediatric experience in Hout Bay, Doctor Billi.

She was really calm and gentle, and I liked her the first time I met her. So, for all the small things, I would go see her, and she was just down the road, which helped. Earlier in the year, we went back to the neurologist (Red Cross doctor), who suggested we start some therapies. We had a hip x-ray done and went to an orthopaedic physician about AFOs.

The AFOs, or ankle and foot orthoses, are little boots which would be moulded and made to fit Ryan's foot and ankle perfectly so that when he wore it, we could get his ankle to 90 degrees, the "normal" position for walking. He had tight muscles and couldn't naturally get into this position. The idea was that the more he wore it, the more it would stretch the tight muscles.

It turned out he was happy to wear them, but trying to find shoes to fit over them was another story!

In February 2005, Ryan had Botox (who knew this was more than a cosmetic solution for everlasting beauty!) to help with the tight muscles in his legs. We also started physio, speech and occupational therapy (O.T.).

By March, Ryan was vomiting again, so we went back to the Red Cross Hospital for a barium swallow and again in May for a milk scan (a dye-like substance that they put down the throat into the stomach to understand the flow of fluids within the body). At this point, we also started getting in night nurses, as Ryan wasn't a great sleeper, and we also needed someone to help out with feeding.

We had tried all sorts of meds to help with Ryan's sleeping, and none of the natural ones worked. We tried a week of Stopayne, which seemed to help, but it caused constipation as it contained codeine. We were already struggling with this, so we soon gave up on the idea.

When we next saw our paediatric neurologist, we mentioned Ryan's sleeping or lack thereof; apparently, children with neurological problems have sleeping problems.

She gave us a script for some sleeping meds and others to help empty the bowel quicker.

The problem was both were syrups in a brown bottle; now, this is where sleep deprivation is very dangerous.

The bowel medicine was 5 ml at a time; the sleeping medication was 2 ml at a time. I gave both medications one night as usual and put Ryan to bed. It was an evening we were on duty to replace the night nurse. Just before bed, I was looking at the bottles, and panic struck. Had I mixed up the doses of the medicines?

Oh my God, yes, I had. I phoned Doctor Billi and tried to tell her what had happened; I don't know how she made sense of it as I was in such a state. She said it was too late to go to the hospital to pump his stomach as it had gone directly into his tummy via the tube. It would have been absorbed quickly. She came over straight away despite it being 11 p.m. She brought some active coal which we syringed into the mickey; now, all we could do was pray it absorbed most of the sleep medicine.

I don't think I slept at all that night. Ryan, on the other hand, slept until lunchtime the next day, and he crapped roads for the whole day.

God, I felt terrible; I very nearly overdosed my son.

In August, we met with a paediatric surgeon, Dr Prof Brown. He, too, was unfamiliar with the peg but had huge experience doing gastrostomies. He was, and still is the most fantastic doctor; his focus was 100% on Ryan during the consultation. He was one of the few medical professionals who showed a genuine interest in Ryan, and his love for children shone from his beaming face. We were reluctant to put Ryan through another surgery, but the mickey button seemed like a more manageable solution. The mickey was also a gastronomy feeding tube but a lot smaller and neater than the peg, and you only attached feeding tubes to it when you needed to; plus, we now had our lovely Doctor Prof Brown to help us. It also meant we didn't have to turn it every hour; we could take it in and out to clean ourselves, and the big plus was that we could get a pump to feed him throughout the night. This potentially meant we would be getting a whole night's sleep when we were on night duty.

When the nurses were there, you would have expected us to pass out, but I think because we had slept so badly for so long, well, mainly me, as I am a light sleeper, we still woke up a lot, and now the nurses had to be trained on the new mickey and new pump so I would be up and showing them how to do it. The feeding pump alarm also went off quite regularly if there was an air bubble or the feeding tube was bent. I'm not sure how I got through all those nights with minimal sleep. I think my body just went into survival mode. In August of that year, he had another dose of Botox and a hearing test, which did not come back normal, but he had just had an ear infection, so we waited for that to be completely clear. Another hearing test came back with negative results in October, but again, he had had an ear infection the month before.

I started hating the Red Cross; you were given an appointment time but waited hours to see the doctor.

You were a number there, not a person. No one cared that you had taken off work and sat in early morning traffic just to make your appointment time, only to wait half a day on a good day to see the person you came to see, and sometimes appointments were only a few minutes with no answers or insight. Unfortunately, because Ryan had so many challenges and did not fit into any box, the doctors weren't sure what to do. It felt like we were living at the Red Cross at times but without the benefit of a comfortable chair/bed and meals. Sometimes, I felt like I was wasting my time and that no good ever came from appointments there.

I felt desperately sorry for those who had gotten up early to take public transport, sometimes travelled for hours, and still had to sit in a packed waiting room for the entire day. You weren't given any respect or special treatment from the staff, but if you were lucky, you got a friendly doctor. We were lucky enough to find a lovely speech therapist there, Vivienne. I really found her so helpful, and she was a great support to me.

In December 2005, she organised a big meeting at the hospital. This included herself, our paed, physio, geneticist(Karen) and a professor of gastrology.

The result of this meeting was that we were to give him more meds to help with his sleeping, and we had to follow up with the Prof in a few weeks. It was at this point we started to understand how tough the road we were on really was. Nothing was straightforward! Although not keen to admit it, the doctors didn't have answers either and were visibly fumbling through potential solutions. It was quite something to see the size of the medical team we had built around ourselves; there were some special people in that team!

The new meds we gave Ryan did not work, so I followed up with the Prof as instructed. I can still remember our conversation so clearly; he never really made eye contact and then said, "Well, that's expected in a child with brain damage."

Wow, was there no other way to put that? Man, could someone please help educate the doctors in the medical profession who lack sympathy and respect? I know they see tough things and deal with very difficult situations, but was a little bit of empathy too much to ask for?

We never went back to that man again. He may have been a professor, but he lacked compassion and people skills, and I have absolutely no respect for him. How dare he speak to us like that? Clearly, he had no clue as to what it was like to have a child that is different.

In Feb 2005, we did a Baer test (hearing test measuring electrical activity in pathways to determine signals between the brain and ear), which did not come back normal, so we then went to an audiologist who did an Auditory Brainstem Response (ABR) test and told us Ryan had profound hearing loss.

I don't have the words to tell you how gutted we were. When she told me, it felt like someone had winded me. I was so angry. Why, why did nothing come back normal? It seemed every appointment we went to resulted in terrible news. I felt defeated and completely flat … like a huge bulldozer had just driven over me … a few times.

The audiologist was very sweet and tried to comfort me, but I remember thinking, *'How can she possibly understand what I am feeling right now? She's probably never had anything bad happen to her.'* About a year later, I discovered she had lost her son a year or two before. I felt absolutely awful for thinking that of her and learnt an invaluable lesson that day: never judge people. You never know what battles they are fighting, despite sometimes thinking they may live with the white picket fence scenario! With Ryan's results, our only option was hearing aids, so we had moulds made, and a week later, we went in to fit them.

It looked like someone had turned the world on. A new universe of sound opened up to our beautiful boy, and the crushing feeling of the test results dissipated as we witnessed the magic of being in a position to provide Ryan with the ability to hear! His little face lit up! We both had tears of joy in our eyes, a point in time I remember as truly incredible. A moment that is etched into my memory bank forever as one of the happiest I have experienced. It was also a very humbling time, another opportunity to recognise and appreciate how lucky we had been up to this point in our lives. Before Ryan, there were no real challenges besides the normal, but nothing that was too much physically or mentally. With Ryan, we had been exposed to almost everything. This was a lesson that was going to be replayed to us many times over the next few years. A lesson that we hold very dear, still to this day.

4

Chapter 4

The Start of School

Lauren

We started at Carel du Toit School for the Deaf a week later. I was super excited; finally, we would get the support we needed. My friend Amy kindly offered to help at my school so I could take the time off to take Ryan. His schooling was a little disturbed due to his having a dose of scarlet fever, ear infections, and tonsillitis in his first month. The plan was to start once a week, as travel time to the school was about an hour each way. We were, nevertheless, hoping this would be a school and social environment Ryan would thrive in. Unfortunately, this was not to be the case. Once it was suspected there was more to Ryan's challenges than just a hearing problem, Carel du Toit informed us their school would not be suitable for Ryan. I was utterly gobsmacked. This was a school for children with challenges, and the minute they heard my son could possibly have a life-limiting syndrome, they threw us out. I would have expected more empathy from them, not to be shown the door. I was so upset! I thought I had found a safe space to be supported but instead was made to feel unwelcome.

Over and above all this, Ryan had his Thyroid tested, which, although typical, showed that he had had CMV at some point.

Of course, once I found that out, I Googled CMV, otherwise known as cytomegalovirus. I thought, *'Oh my God, this is it; we have a diagnosis for Ryan'.* I managed to find other Mommies with CMV babies and started feeling like I had found a real support group, finally people who could truly understand our daily struggles.

February was a busy month; Ryan had bronchitis, and Botox was administered again, but this time, they followed the Botox up by putting his legs in casts to try and stretch the ligaments to induce better flexibility. This would improve muscle tone, enabling him to move more freely. He was in these casts (both legs) for 6 weeks, and it was a proper mission…true to Ryan style, though he just got on with things and barely moaned about it, choosing instead to smile and laugh his way through his difficulties (at least that is what it seemed). Ryan, through everything, had an uncanny ability to communicate his emotions: happiness, mischievousness, and fun. He had a few signals that also told us when he was unhappy, like a hand or, even worse, 2 hands up on his forehead, which essentially meant F-you or F-off. These did not come often, but when they arrived, and his beautiful smile was replaced by that frown and hands on his face, you knew he was not messing about. We first noticed his distress signal after his MRI scan, early in life, and then again after the casts were put on.

Feeding was supposed to be easier now that we had the mickey, but Ryan was struggling with his weight, and for those first three years, he had remained at 7 kgs. We tried all sorts of milk. The first dietician suggested we give him one cup of olive oil daily. Thinking back, I really should have reported her to someone as, firstly, how can a child have so much olive oil and secondly, in a child of Ryan's size? It would have made him seriously ill. We were then referred to another dietician at the Red Cross who suggested a milk called Frebeeni energy fibre; it came measured out in little bags and was high in calories and high in price.

After fighting with our medical aid, they eventually agreed to pay for it, and we had decided that when Ryan put on weight, we would celebrate, so we excitedly started the milk. Before we knew it, Ryan was up to 10 kgs. What a celebration! My aunt organised a brunch for my whole family, and we had a 10 kg party!!

Rejoice in the little things!!

2006 was all about testing and hearing. I will never forget sitting in the neurologist's room at the Red Cross when she dropped a bombshell.

"Lauren, I feel we need to do more tests for Angelman."

It seemed CMV had been forgotten, and suddenly, C.P. was not a diagnosis anymore. I liked this Doctor, but I thought, *'Do these doctors know what they are doing?'* I sat there in total disbelief. Part of me wanted to cry, but I also didn't want to panic about something that might not be true. They cannot suggest my son has a life-threatening genetic syndrome. They said it was C.P. and it wouldn't happen again. This cannot be happening; I have to tell the doctor. I'm 6 weeks pregnant!!

Paul

Deciding to try for a second child was a huge decision and not taken lightly. Although Ryan had been diagnosed with "C.P." and CMV, obviously, there was anxiety. So when we found out we were pregnant with our second child, we had mixed emotions. We were excited but, in the back of our minds, also a bit worried. Now the Doctors were talking about Ryan as having a genetic syndrome, which could mean the new baby might have it too. We had some potentially tough decisions to make but avoided discussing any of them as we concluded that if our 2nd child had the same syndrome, we at least were in a position where we knew what to expect and how to handle it!

Lauren

After telling the doctor I was pregnant and discussing all the options, we decided to test Ryan, but we were not going to test the baby until we had results for Ryan as it was too risky for the baby. What a day!! I fucking hate the Red Cross. Every time I go to that damn hospital, I make sure I have my angry music with me because I am angry, sad, disappointed, gutted, and shattered every time I leave there. Only Eminem helps!

For the rest of that day and the next, I kind of went into a dark space where everything was overwhelming and sad, but after a day or two, I felt fine again. Friends and family know not to phone me on these days as I am a mess, have headaches, am emotionally exhausted, and am just plain old miserable.

As mentioned already, I Googled and tried everything with Ryan. We started hydrotherapy as we thought the warm water would help release his tight muscles, but unfortunately, it didn't work as Ryan kept getting pneumonia.

One day, a friend and I went to a SARDA (South African Riding for the Disabled Association) market; I had never been there before, so I decided to go check it out. We walked around the stalls and saw they offered horse rides, so we asked if Ryan could have a go. He was only 3 at the time, so they were a bit hesitant but put him on.

Oh my gosh, I will never forget the look on his little face; he was absolutely thrilled with himself and loved it. Afterwards, I went to chat with the person in charge. There was space for him, but only for a few months. So, on 3 May 2006, our amazing SARDA journey started. We would be in Margaret's class and go every Wednesday for an hour, and Ryan loved every minute of it. He looked like he felt that he was such a big and important boy (which, of course, he was).

He would tell his horse, which was the same one every week, to walk, and we would do all sorts of exercises. Myself and Amy would walk beside him, and the horse had a leader.

Ryan's first horse was named Kwela, but after about a year, Kwela retired, and then he had Panache Firefly, otherwise known as Flea. The one lesson we tried to put him on another horse, and he would have none of it! The horse riding gave Ryan a sense of independence. He absolutely loved every minute of it. He was in charge for that hour and told the horse what to do. His most favourite thing in the world was to trot, and even though it looked like his little head would fall off his neck, he had the biggest smile! Not only did he love it, but he didn't realise how good it was for him to have his legs stretched in that position; it was a win-win!

Another huge accomplishment which happened in 2006 was the day I put Ryan on the little black scooter at my school; I thought it would be good for his legs and hips as you must sit with your thighs apart. I was busy with the other children, and when I looked up, Ryan was not where I had parked him; he was down on the other side of the playground. I asked the teachers and the children, and they all said they had not moved him. I was puzzled but brought him back up to where we were. The next thing he started moving and pushing himself on the bike. I could not believe my eyes. I cannot tell you how incredibly proud I was of my boy; this was unbelievable. I took hundreds of photos and phoned everyone to tell them. What an amazing day!

The next appointment we had was to have Ryan's eyesight tested. We weren't worried but figured we had done every other test; we might as well rule it out. Surprise, surprise, the test came back that he needed glasses. I almost just laughed; of course, he needed glasses. Nothing came back normal! At this stage, I had started focusing on the positives: how cute would he look with glasses? So off I went to choose spectacles for our tiny 3-year-old, and oh my gosh, I didn't think he could get cuter, but I was so wrong!!

Paul

A few days after Ryan got his new specs, we had an assessment at Vista Nova. I was a little worried as he had a bad chest again.

It was a tough day for me. I had grown up in Pinelands, which was not too far from Vista Nova and had seen many of the kids that went to the school as a child. These days, I think we have conditioned our kids to be far more accepting of children with challenges, but in my day, we either ignored them or kind of mocked them (horrible and cruel, I know - but this is the honest truth). Here I was, a sport and businessman with the world at my feet, taking my child to a school I had thought so little of as a child. Not the plan I had had in mind, not in my wildest thinking. I walked into the school and felt angry at having to be there. So far, this was the most challenging task I had to do with my son. More than any operation or other disappointment we had been through, I always believed that my Tiger would be okay and that these guys had got it all wrong. In a way, I think this was a watershed moment for me to help come to terms with the fact that my son was different and had special needs. It was not easy for me to digest, but I sucked it up and knew we had to do what was best and right for Ryan, that was for sure, and I needed to get over myself and my prejudices.

He went to school for his first day. It was a disaster, and we were dropped another bombshell. The school told us they didn't think he would cope. It was not the school for Ryan. We needed to look at other options for more "severe" kids.

'How dare they judge our son like that', I thought. Lauren and I were utterly heartbroken. I nearly hit the roof, or maybe I did. What were they saying? I could not accept he needed to go there, and now he was not good enough for them. The impossible had happened. Not even Vista Nova would take my beautiful boy. I was convinced they were not giving him a chance and must have mixed him up with some other child. The reality of Ryan's situation was becoming ever more apparent. It is truly amazing how one sees situations and circumstances from completely different perspectives, depending on whether you are looking in or out. Take the example of a friend dating a girl. He might be completely in love at the time, but all his mates can see she is totally wrong for him; no matter what you say, he won't listen. Then the inevitable happens: they break up, and he sees it from a completely

different perspective, realising that she was entirely wrong for him. I think this was my reality at the time with Nova Vista, my boy and my broken heart.

I went from thinking our son would go to a top boy's school to finding out that even a school for kids with learning disabilities wouldn't take him. I was destroyed. *'They clearly didn't know what they were talking about. Were they talking about the right child?'* I thought to myself. *'Our beautiful Ryan? Surely not; how can no one see what we see?'*

That week, we investigated all possible options. Lauren phoned local schools and was horrified at their reactions. We even explored options in Joburg. An option I could work with but one that frightened Lauren. I knew she had to be really concerned to even think about Joburg as an option since she did not enjoy our last stint there. Just goes to show the depth of love one can have for a child and what lengths you will go to for them. This may not have seemed like a big thing to many, but for Lauren, family is everything, and her family was all in Cape Town.

Some people suggested Bel Porto, a school for children with intellectual impairment, cerebral palsy and/or physical disabilities. Still, there was no way we would send our boy there. We reluctantly put his name on the waiting list and decided to park the Joburg idea for a while. At least in Cape Town, we had fantastic support through friends and family, which counted for an immeasurable amount.

In 2007, we got a call to say Bel Porto had a place for our son. Lauren thanked them very much but declined the position. We both felt it wasn't the place for him. For me, it was a horrifying idea. The facilities were poor, and it was for kids with severe difficulties. Our Tiger was not in this category. It was certainly as far as you could get from any top boy's school. After months of looking for alternatives, we realised we didn't have a choice, so we had to put our pride in our pocket and phone Bel Porto back, asking if they still had the space for Ryan. So, at the beginning of 2008, Ryan started at Bel Porto. I was sure my boy would demonstrate to these guys they had made a judgment error, and he would be sent to Vista Nova soon anyway. That was my thinking; it was what I was holding onto.

Lauren

When the first day of school arrived, we tried to be excited. The one fun project was that we bought Ryan the uniform, which was ridiculously cute as Ryan was only the size of an 18-month-old.

He looked super chuffed in his navy shorts, white shirt with the Bel Porto badge on it, white takkies and socks and his wheely bag, which was pretty much the same size as him. I packed him a lunch box filled with snacks, fruit, bite-size sandwiches and raisins, hoping the school would help with his feeding.

I will never ever forget reading his message book at the end of his first day of school."Ryan ate one raisin today."

Wow, what a day, one raisin! The Spagnoletti motto became *'rejoice in the little things, even if the little thing is one raisin.'*

Bel Porto was a good 40 minutes away from where we lived, and because my school started so early, it was pretty tricky working out the lifts. Paul would take Ryan to my mom, and she would take him to school as she worked close by. I would fetch him after lunch as my work was quieter then.

Ryan was a super friendly and very social little guy, but boy, did he take a long time to settle into school. Every morning for weeks, he would make himself vomit (his party trick when he was trying to get out of something) on the way to school. My mom would wipe him down and drop him off. I think he thought he was too big for school and wanted to be with his mommy!!

Ryan soon became very popular and well-liked at Bel Porto. He was the tiniest little kiddie by far, and everyone knew who he was. He had the staff wrapped around his little finger.

The children in his class were terrific with him. They would help him get in his chair for ring time and push him in his buggy to assembly, and when I arrived to fetch him, there was a scramble to see who could get his bag first.

Although Ryan made many friends at school, we never had playdates and were never social with the parents at Bel Porto, as many children came from very different backgrounds. Even the R170 monthly school fees were too much for many of them to pay, so even though we now had a school for Ryan, I felt pretty alone on his journey. I also think for Paul, it was easier not to engage with other parents as it was his way of not genuinely accepting the situation as it was. In Ryan, we had our world and lived in our cocoon with our trusted friends and family, and while we were acutely aware of Ryan's challenges, we just continued life as if they weren't there. For Paul, engaging with children with similar challenges was an admission of the situation, so burying his head in the sand (ostrich scenario) was safer and easier. I, on the other hand, was better at dealing with the reality of the situation, and my thirst for information to help my boy always enabled me to face the harsh realities of what we were dealing with, engaging with parents and medical people. We genuinely believe our differences in how we met the circumstances were our strength. We complemented each other, taking turns to be the one of strength and positivity depending on our situations.

After school, there was a designated sleep time, but Ryan never lay down and slept; he made his own rules. Soon after he started school, the school physio, Jenny, suggested getting some equipment to help him. We went to a company called Shonaquip; they do all sorts of equipment for disabled children. It was terrific; we put him in a buggy, which is like a wheelchair but with big wheels. It had enough support in the right places for him to sit correctly. Within minutes of being in the buggy, he started moving it; there was tremendous excitement and teary eyes. We then tried him in a standing walker, where he would be strapped into a standing position. It also had big wheels to push, and he moved this one so quickly. Seeing him in these was the best thing; he had such a sense of independence. Luckily, medical aid paid for the equipment, which came close to R10,000. We also got a walking frame for him, like the ones old people use. So he was fully kitted out!

It wasn't practical for us to use the medical equipment at home as he was so small, so we just used his pram and carried him everywhere; luckily, the big equipment could stay at school. It was at this point that we changed physios. The physio we had been seeing was over half an hour away from us, so when we found out Jenny did home visits, it was a no-brainer. She started coming once a week to our house to do the physio, which Ryan hated.

He would make himself vomit, scream and cry before she had even started. Sometimes, he would try to hide, but he would usually see her coming, waving, saying goodbye, and blowing her kisses.

It was heartbreaking to watch, but I knew he had to do it; the more stretches he did, the better for him.

His second year at Bel Porto was better, and he was settled; he knew everyone and his routine. He really became Mr. Popular.

He then moved to the "big" class. It became clear to us that Ryan's time would be limited at Bel Porto because he couldn't do everything the other children could, but until then, we wouldn't stress about it. The foundation phase held a concert in his first year of big class (2010). Ryan was chosen to be a sleeping cow. He wore black and white and had a tail and horns. He was the most beautiful sleeping cow I have ever seen. After the concert, they all sang the national anthem, and when I looked over at Ryan, he was in one of the teacher's arms, with his hand on his heart. I will never forget that beautiful image of my boy.

Paul

By this stage, I realised the idea of Ryan going to Vista Nova and the wrong assessment was not a reality. As Lauren mentioned, it was a matter of how long he could stay at Bel Porto! However, we were now more used to his environment and could see how much Ryan was loved at the school. That was the most important thing. He was, for the most part, year 2 onward, happy and was always the centre of attention, which was where he loved to be most ☺.

That place was amazing. I had always expected to be on the side of a sports field watching my son excel in a sporting discipline, and here I was bursting with pride at him being a sleeping cow in a play. Again, this is a testament to us learning very quickly to celebrate the little things and all the achievements, no matter how small.

Ryan always had an innate ability to tune into the core of things and, despite his challenges, could articulate and appreciate situations around him. Like the anthem, knowing to put his tiny hand to his heart and singing away in his little voice that nobody could understand beside him. His eyes and smile would always tell you how he felt or his ability to draw people to him and see into someone's soul. This gift will always amaze me—the magic of my darling boy.

5

Chapter 5

And Then There Were Two

Lauren

Deciding to have a second baby was a huge decision, but as soon as we had decided, I found myself pregnant. We changed doctors as I wasn't happy with how my previous gynae had dealt with the end of my pregnancy. New gynae, new hospital, new baby! And Amy was pregnant too! It turned out our babies were due a few days apart.

How awesome having someone pregnant with me this time. I loved telling people I was pregnant. Well, most people. When one of my uncles found out I was pregnant, he asked if this baby was going to be normal. What the f###? What is normal anyway?

I bought a t-shirt for Ryan saying *'I'm the big brother'* and showed my mom, who was ecstatic. My dad was the only person who didn't want to know the sex, so keeping a secret from one person was quite tricky.

We decided to find out the sex immediately, although we knew that the chances of it being a boy were very high. So, at 11 weeks, to no one's surprise, it was confirmed we were having another boy. The big boy name debate started again. Paul liked the name Sergio, heaven help us.

I liked Matthew (although there was already a Matthew Spagnoletti, who we seldom saw), Jayden and Jordy. I had very little morning sickness, which was great! All was looking good until that dreaded 28 weeks when the doctors started getting concerned about baby's growth. Again, I was ordered bed rest. Unfortunately, because of my reaction to the steroids last time, they were not happy to give them to me again, so we just had to pray that this time the baby would stay in for longer. Luckily, me being me, I was pretty organised. The nursery was almost ready. We had chosen a jungle theme, and I had painted light green halfway up the wall, with animals bordering the top. We still had Ryan's clothes, which had been washed and packed in the cupboard. No sewing for me this time, so I bought a cot duvet cover and bumper.

Christmas was around the corner, so when my cousin organised a Christmas party on 10 December, I thought nothing of it. I wasn't feeling great that day, so I messaged her and had a sleep but decided to go even though we were quite late. As soon as we arrived, I saw all the cars and knew something was up. It was my baby shower. I got spoilt again, and it was such a lovely day. All the little blue outfits were so cute; we left there with a car full of presents.

At my next appointment, my gynae decided I needed a Caesar sooner than we had originally thought. She told us we could have Christmas at home, but I had to come into the hospital the next day. After the appointment, I went up to see the neonatal unit to have a look and meet the nurses, as I knew too well we would be spending lots of time there. I rang the bell, and the nurse opened the door. I explained that I would have my baby early and wanted to look around. She explained I should keep my baby in for as long as possible and try not to have a premature birth. *'Hello lady, like I have a choice?'* I thought to myself and then explained in a very nice way this was my second baby and that my first was prem, so I knew all about prem babies. She quickly changed her tune, and we actually got on really well after that.

We had a lovely Christmas lunch, and Ryan went home with my mom as he was going to sleep there. All of a sudden, a strange feeling came over me, a feeling of sadness for Ryan; our boy was not going to know what had hit him. He had been the only child for over 3 years, and all of a sudden, he would have to share us. Could I love another child like I loved Ryan? Although I felt rather anxious, I slept relatively well that night. On our way to the hospital the next morning, I phoned Sylvia and wished her a happy birthday. I felt calm but excited; I would meet my second son today! At least this time, I knew what to expect from the caesar, but our anxiety was the unknown of our boy's health. Even though the Doctors still did not have an official diagnosis for Ryan and said it probably wouldn't happen again, we were nervous.

I had been very happy with my new gynae so far, and she had recommended a paediatrician who, unfortunately, was on leave, so we got another very nice doctor. Paul's intentions were to be standing right next to me, front row, watching everything. Still, within two minutes of the gynae starting, there was a burning smell, and after discovering it was me having my last Caesar scar lasered, Paul didn't feel too well, and the nurses had to hurry to get him a chair and some sugar water.

Paul

I was much calmer and more relaxed throughout the second pregnancy. I distinctly remember Lauren saying to me, "But what happens if our 2nd child has the same challenges as Ryan?" My response was, "Well, at least we have experience with it and know what to do."

From 28 weeks, the anxiety and tension could be cut with a knife. There were those mixed feelings again, the stress and excitement at the prospect of having another boy.

Much to my disappointment, Lauren won the name battle, but I also thought Matthew was beautiful. It was interesting; many people don't find out the sex of their baby, so they still have a surprise on the day, and many have anxiety about whether it is a boy or a girl. Not many parents have to worry so much about their child's health. In our case, this was our reality, and the anxiety was whether our boy would be a healthy "normal" baby or have challenges like his brother.

The day had come.

You might remember that after Lauren gave birth to Ryan, I enjoyed the experience so much that I was willing to play dad for the day for anyone. But not this time. I nearly didn't make it through the birth, and to be honest, I am not sure how I didn't faint; the sight of that smoke and the smell of burning skin, hell's bells, how about some warning next time, peeps? But I did make it, and what a day! Our 2nd son had arrived into the world!

Lauren

The baby started crying as soon as he was born, which was music to our ears.

We found out later in the day that there was no fluid left for the baby, so taking him out early had been imperative. Because there was no fluid when the gynae cut me open, she cut his little bottom, too; no wonder he came out crying!! He had a little Zorro scar on his bottom, which they quickly steri-stripped together. They weighed him and did all the tests. I was so happy he was bigger than we thought he was going to be. Matthew James Spagnoletti (James was my Dad's second name) was born on 26 December 2006 and weighed 1,9 kgs. They put him on my chest, and I stared at our beautiful baby boy, but within a few minutes, he started blowing bubbles, indicating that he wasn't breathing well. So, once again, my new baby was whisked off to the neonatal unit.

The hospital staff were lovely; luckily, I had a private room this time, so I didn't have to have mommies with their new babies in the room with me. Unfortunately, my family came to visit but couldn't see Matthew, so I remember loading all my photos onto my laptop and showing them pics of him. Matthew was on oxygen for a week and in an incubator for nearly 8 days, and it felt very déjà vu'ish, us not being able to hold our baby, but at least this time, we were prepared. It felt very normal for us to have babies we couldn't hold straight away. I knew the drill, so I started expressing milk straight away, and Matthew seemed to be doing well. He definitely wasn't as sick as Ryan had been. That New Year's Eve, we went to see friends without our new baby, and there I sat every three hours, expressing milk. By this stage, we were very used to the hospital situation. I would spend part of the day at the hospital, expressing and trying to do kanga care and the other half with Ryan. Luckily, it was the December holidays, so we had lots of support.

We got to hold Matthew when he was one week old, and once he was off oxygen, Ryan was allowed to come and meet his little brother, who he thought was very funny. He clearly didn't realise Matthew was here to stay and disrupt his little single-child world!

By this stage, Deon, the paediatrician our gynae had recommended, was back from leave. On 8 January, he told us Matthew could go home if he maintained his weight overnight with me feeding him. So, on the 9th of January, I went back to the hospital to spend the night with my boy, again we told no one. And yes, on the 10th of January, Matthew came home. We settled into being a family of four very quickly, and Ryan was very taken with this new being in our midst.

At about two months, I started to notice Matthew didn't seem to focus as well as he should and thought I saw a milky film over his eyes. I made an appointment to see Deon, and it was confirmed Matthew had cataracts. I remember leaving the hospital in tears and phoning Paul on my way out. Why was this happening to us?

We were referred to an ophthalmologist to explore our next step.

It was decided that Matthew would need both lenses removed, but one at a time. Thereafter, he would need to wear 200+ contact lenses. It all seemed just too much; how were we going to cope with this? So, our tiny little 3-month-old (weighing only 3 kgs) went in to have one eye done. The op went well, and he came home with a little eye patch. A few weeks later, he went in to have the other one done.

Once things were settled, we went to the eye clinic at the Red Cross to get help with the contact lenses.

Red Cross again, we couldn't seem to get rid of the place. It was agreed we would put the contacts in at the hospital and come back every two weeks to change them, and after a few weeks of this, Paul and I would have to try and do it ourselves. So, I had to keep my nails very short and put my big girl panties on.

I would sit over Matthew so only his tiny head showed, and Paul would open his eyes then I would try and get it out. It was not an easy task to perform on a tiny baby. Taking them out was okay, but putting them back in came with more challenges. At times, they would get stuck to his eyelid, and then we would have to try and move them. It was extremely stressful, plus each lens was about R1000, so you really didn't want to lose them.

The one thing that stands out for me is that Matthews' eyes, with the contact lenses in, were a bright, beautiful, shiny blue.

Paul

I remember the horror. I had to pin my child down whilst he was screaming blue murder and forcing his eyes open to get the contacts in. It was a nightmare and really hard to do. It never got easier, mostly due to Matthew's trauma and the stress it placed on Lauren and me. Looking back, I still can't believe we did this for 18 months. During this time, we started discovering Matthew didn't seem to handle the sun or heat very well. Living in a warm and sunny climate like South Africa was less than ideal. The reality of this challenge became evident on one holiday in Hermanus (a seaside village 90 minutes outside of Cape Town), where we had gone away with friends. We spent the day on the water in their boat, playing on an island beach, skiing, and having a great time. Nevertheless, we got back to the house and were playing in the garden and noticed Matthew's eyes started to swell.

Being proactive and having a 6th sense for situations like this, Lauren immediately said we needed to head back to Cape Town. We decided we better get his contacts out first, and it was then we realised the enormity of the situation as we could not open his eyes due to the swelling of his face. We rushed back to Cape Town and straight to the Emergency room. It was quite a palaver, and just explaining to the on-duty doctors that Matthew had contact lenses was a process. Let's face it; this is not something they hear every day and have to deal with, especially with a little child, exaggerated by the fact that Matthew was smaller by some margin than boys of a similar age to him. It was all very complicated, and the process to get it sorted meant the stress we were under now moved onto a completely new level.

The doctor on call wanted to use paper clips to keep Matthew's eyes open so we could attempt to get his lenses out. We were bewildered and so nervous. In the end, we decided to leave them in as it would have been too traumatic for everyone to attempt that.

After that nightmare scenario, we were extremely careful with Matthew and his exposure to heat or sun. This became a continual battle for us, as naturally, he loved being outside. We knew we had to do something that would alleviate the pain of taking his contacts in and out and reduce the risks associated with swelling from heat and the sun. Fortunately, Lauren, who is persistent, convinced our doctor that Matthew was ready for a lens implant.

I had hoped we would experience the same magic we had witnessed when Ryan got hearing aids, but alas, we did not. Matthew would still have to wear glasses, but at least we had removed the trauma of the contact routine for both Matthew and ourselves by having the implants, so it's still a big win in our books!

6

Chapter 6

The Diagnosis

Lauren

After the lens implant, the strangest thing happened: Matthew's bright blue eyes changed to a grey/green colour.

Unfortunately, the lens implants did not give Matthew 100% vision, so he still had to wear the thickest glasses I had ever seen; they made Ryan's glasses look thin in comparison.

Cataracts led Karen, our geneticist, down a different path, and she told me she thought our boys might have a syndrome called Cockayne Syndrome, and if it weren't that, it would be a similar syndrome. I, of course, Googled it as soon as I put the phone down: "Cockayne Syndrome is a rare disorder characterised by an abnormally small head size (microcephaly), a failure to gain weight and grow (failure to thrive), leading to very short stature and delayed development and premature ageing resulting in a shortened life span, about 5-7 years." What? Did I just read that both my boys were only going to live 5–7 years?

It had taken us so long to accept that we had one child with special needs, and we were only just beginning to find our way with Ryan. Now, we may have two, both potentially with a shortened life; this couldn't be happening. This was not what I had planned for my family; the pain in my chest was so sore I couldn't breathe. I started panicking and hyperventilating.

How was I going to tell Paul and the rest of our family?

Paul

I got home that night to a devastated wife and mother. She explained to me about the conversation between her and Karen and her findings through her research. What does one say? Well, if I had been in denial before, there was now no way I was going to escape this reality and the enormity of our situation. It was a hard pill to swallow. A reality of such uncertainty and pain. What sort of lives would our gorgeous and beloved children now lead?

To be honest, I realised the struggles were mine and Lauren's. For Ryan and Matthew, this was their reality and all they knew in life. It was what it was.

Lauren

Soon after hearing that Ryan and Mathew may have CS, I emailed a professor at Harvard, Prof Neilan, who was mentioned on the internet and explained my situation to him.

To my surprise, he responded and offered to do testing for free for research purposes. Part of this meant he couldn't give me official results, only a yes or no answer. That did not bother us. We just wanted a result (little did we know that we would need official results a few years later).

I contacted Karen and told her all about Doctor Neilan, and they got in contact.

He would need skin, hair, and blood to be sent over to him.

We decided to take the samples from Matthew as Ryan had been through so much testing already, and Matthew was due to have a general anaesthetic anyway as he was just about to have a 'mickey' put in.

While we were waiting for results, I went onto the '*Amy and friends*' and '*Share and Care*' websites and read all about CS.

They had a page with pictures of the kids and a little write-up on each child.

I remember thinking, '*Wow, some of these kiddies look just like my boys.*'

A few families with siblings had CS, and two boys really stuck out for me, Alexander and Jacob; they were brothers and looked very similar to my boys. Could we have a diagnosis for our boys after nearly four years of not knowing?

That year, Paul and I had planned our first overseas trip together; I was beyond excited. It was going to be my first overseas trip, and it couldn't have come at a better time. When we decided that we wanted to make an overseas trip, the first question that came up was, to where?? As I had never been overseas, there seemed to be so many options, but as I am quite money-conscious, I wanted to go somewhere where our currency wasn't totally useless. Hence, we eventually decided on Thailand. Our Rand was stronger, and Thailand was going to be so culturally different for us.

We were leaving on 27 June and would land in Bangkok on 28 June, my birthday!!

Birthdays are a huge deal for me. I start counting days, even months before and basically have a birthday month with lots of celebrations, so for me to be away for my birthday was a huge thing, but it was going to be amazing.

It was the first time we were leaving the boys for so long, but I knew they would be fine as my mom, sister, and Paul's parents would be looking after them. Plus, Paul and I needed this; we needed a break from reality, even if it was only for a few days.

I made lists upon lists for them with instructions for feeding, sleeping, school, doctors' numbers, and medical aid details. I phoned the doctors and told them we were going to be away and that the family were looking after the boys. There was so much to plan and prepare. Our introduction to Parenthood started with a bang and didn't ease up, so it was nice for us as a couple to have some time to connect again.

Paul

The trip to Thailand was a special time for me and Lauren. We could just be ourselves for a time, not worry (too much) about all the stresses of life. We did not do Thailand on the cheap; we went all out and made it a really awesome holiday, having a hotel on a private beach, doing all the tourist things, riding elephants, temples, Thai-Boxing, night-life adventures, kayaking, snorkelling and touring islands. We made incredible memories, reconnecting with each other and enjoying our own company. We visited Bangkok and Phuket. This was Lauren's first trip overseas, and the East was a perfect choice. It is hard to beat the magical land of Thailand as your first adventure. There is no doubt the travel bug bit and hard ☺

Lauren

After what seemed to take an eternity, Karen phoned to say she had the results, and we had to come in to discuss them. That didn't sound good, but in my heart, I knew it was Cockayne Syndrome, as the boys had all the symptoms and looked identical to the other children.

Nevertheless, I cried when I found out they were positive for type 2 Cockayne Syndrome; I'm not sure if it was because of the actual result or from relief we now had an answer. We could finally move on, and I could stop looking for answers.

Along our journey to finding a diagnosis, I met so many parents of special needs children, some making a bigger impact than others. I remember chatting with a mom and noticing her tattoo. When I asked her about it, she said once she found out her son was not going to live for long, she decided she needed a tattoo of his name. Wow, it was such a surreal moment, and I remember thinking, if that happened to me, I would do the same. This stuck in the back of my mind until I got the official diagnosis, and then, telling no one, I went to get my first tattoo. I chose to have it on the inside of my left wrist, where I could see it daily. I chose an R and an M.

I remember how shocked everyone was. It was something I felt I needed to do and treasure every day.

After the diagnosis, life took a surprising turn for the better. I was relieved to have an answer and put the limited life part of the diagnosis deep in my subconscious. We always joked we had the most expensive no-name brands. Now we had a name.

My journey with CS began with Google and led me down a trail that would take me halfway around the world, meet other incredibly rare CS children and be part of the futuristic research into this genetic syndrome to help change lives.

I was contacted by Haylee, founder of the Facebook group, Share and Care (a CS support group in the United States), after I told them my story. Haylee phoned me, and I will never forget our conversation. She was telling me about her daughter, Eden, who had CS, and I was blown away. She told me Eden had chubby little fingers and podgy little toes and that her feet were always cold, even in socks, exactly like Ryan's. I became friends with her on Facebook after that, and there were so many similarities between Eden and Ryan.

Haylee had had another son called Ian, and although he hadn't been diagnosed when he passed away, they suspected Ian had had CS too.

I remember thinking; my boys will be different; they won't die young.

She told me about a medical conference they hold every year in the States, where they sponsored families to come. Still, it was too late for us that year as all the families were already organised, but she mentioned another group I should contact.

So I contacted *Amy and Friends* in the UK and spoke to their founder, Jayne; they also sponsored families to come to their retreat and said she would do her best to get us there, fully paid.

Wow, can you believe it? I had found other CS children and families and, in a few months, could possibly be meeting them.

The rest of 2008 was spent doing weight, height and head circumference measurements every month.

The teacher in me came out guns blazing; I had a plan and knew what had to be done.

In August, Matthew got pneumonia and RSV (Respiratory Syncytial Virus - which causes infections of the lungs and respiratory tract), and we were in the hospital for 3 very long weeks.

Having a child in the hospital is no easy thing with work commitments, plus having Ryan, who was also immune-compromised, so he couldn't afford to get sick.

We had a hospital plan where Paul would sleep at the hospital, and then either Paul's parents or I would go there in the morning, and we would swap for the afternoon shift.

My mom and sister would come in the early evening so Paul, Ryan, and I could have dinner together, and then Paul would go back to the hospital to sleep. It wasn't ideal, but given the circumstances, it worked.

Thankfully, the staff at the hospital were lovely, especially Trudy. If we needed anything, she would help, and she made Matthew feel very loved and us very welcome.

Matthew was a ladies' man, our lover, and soon he had a "wife" at the hospital. Joyce, one of the nurses who he absolutely loved. When Matthew saw her, his eyes would brighten, his little face would beam, and he would reach out to her like she was his most precious treasure.

Remember her name and his love for her; I will mention her again.

Paul

The good news was that we could now care for them in a way that fitted their needs as opposed to always guessing. It was also a time of growth as we could now compare notes with parents of other kids with CS. They had very similar challenges, so we were not alone anymore. I guess one of the biggest realisations was that the group of kids we had as a reference point was rare. There were only a hundred known cases of CS in the world. In South Africa, there were a whopping zero other known cases. In time, we discovered one other case in Kwazulu Natal (East coast of South Africa), but that was some years later, as well as potential other cases in Cape Town. Still, they were not prepared to have it confirmed, so by all accounts, there were 2 cases of CS in South Africa during the lifespan of our boys. These were shocking and humbling statistics for us.

The positive side would be the possible trips to Europe. Lauren and I both liked to travel, so this was a good reason to fly to Europe annually for the conferences.

Another wonderful discovery was how unbelievably amazing Deon and Karen led our medical team. It had taken a lot of time and pain to reach a point where we found a medical team that embraced our situation, dedicated themselves to our children and became an extension of our family. The hospital became a home away from home, and we would spend an enormous amount of time at Cape Town Medi-Clinic in the coming years. Our doctors would often be ahead of their counterparts in the States and Europe, yet they only had one case to work from. It was quite incredible; we were so blessed to have such a wonderful team supporting us.

So, to put things in context and build a picture of what our two awesome boys were dealing with, here is a list .... Are you ready:

- Microcephaly (small head)
- Growth challenges (small stature, neither boy got bigger than a 2-3-year-old)
- Lack of movement – Ryan could bum-shuffle, and Matthew could crawl – both could ride a black 3-wheel scooter bike
- Poor vision – Both wore glasses
- Poor eating – Both had eating tubes, so they were fed via a pump at night with liquid food; they would not even eat chocolate.
- Poor hearing – Both wore hearing aids
- Lack of communication ability – Both had a few words; they used sounds and hand gestures to communicate, but boy, did you know what they wanted.
- Loss of hair – More related to Ryan
- Poor teeth
- Fast ageing – became little old men, more so Ryan than Matthew.
- High-muscle tone – leads to limited mobility and fine motor skills.
- Sensitivity to heat – More Matthew than Ryan
- Vomiting – More Ryan than Matthew

- Poor sleeping rhythms
- Limited lifespan

I am not sure there was much more on the Cockayne Syndrome (CS) list that a child could have; our boys had about it all. But they were the happiest and friendliest children I knew! Ryan had such a cute sense of humour. He could be rather naughty and cheeky. A lovely memory of Ryan's mischievousness was having dinner at my parent's house one night. Ryan was sitting beside my mom when he knocked a napkin off the table. As she bent down to pick it up, he bonked her on the head with a spoon and burst into laughter, which was extra cute coming from this tiny little "voice." Matthew loved hair and would give out incredible hugs, holding a person with such an intensity you felt he would never let go. At the same time (if you had long hair), he would nibble on a ponytail; the dogs also had their ears nibbled on by Matti. I was amazed at how patient our dog was with him. Chloe, our Lab/Ridgeback mix, was so wonderful with Matthew. Matthew would crawl up to her and pull her tail and bite her ears, and she would do nothing; they had a 6th sense around the boys.

Observing the similarities and differences between our two boys was interesting as time went by. Both were dealing with CS, with similarities in the eating, seeing and hearing challenges, but like most siblings, different in other ways. Ryan was never able to get past the bum-shuffling stage; Matti, on the other hand, was able to crawl. The day that happened was a momentous occasion for us. So we had another of those Spagnoletti celebrations, a growing tradition now where we rejoiced in those enormous small things our beautiful boys achieved. Matti was two years old, and Lauren and I were over the moon. We started to believe our boy would one day be able to walk; he had achieved a traditional milestone, something we rarely experienced. Although Ryan had never crawled, he once took three to four steps across the living room at Lauren's mom's house. Unfortunately, this was never to be repeated despite months of encouraging efforts. Matti, on the other hand, had actually crawled. Could he beat the odds and show the world that even with CS type 2, he could become mobile? We had such high hopes at the time. I wish I could tell you our boy did end up walking. But he didn't. So we moved on through another of our many broken dreams and, in our endearing optimism, were delighted and so proud of our little boy for accomplishing this wonderful ability to move reasonably freely. Like Ryan, he loved riding his bike, which gave them both a great sense of freedom.

It must have been hard for our friends; we lost contact with many people along the journey. I can understand why, I guess. It's not easy when you have healthy kids who can do all the "normal" things, and you have people around who have kids who can't. Sometimes, the reality of it was too much for some people, and "friends" became simply acquaintances. But in saying that, we were also wonderfully blessed to have some incredible true friends who looked past our kid's inabilities and challenges and saw the boys for who they were, celebrating their achievements with us; this would define our strongest friendships. This group of people were a great part of our source of strength and supported us through thick and thin. Duncan and Amy were with us every step of our journey, from bringing us meals in the hospital to helping Lauren at work so she could go to doctors' appointments. They were the first people at the hospital in our darkest hours and the last to leave if we needed them. John and Sylvia were a phone call away and provided huge amounts of support.

We have always mentioned how supportive and lovely our respective families were. It seems no better time than now to call out my parents and their wonderful support through everything. They had the luxury of being able to help at SARDA (South African Riding for the Disabled Association) a lot and still help there, I guess as a way of dedication to the boys. Lauren's mom, sister Shelly and Lionel were always there for us and were a massive support for us both, providing babysitting at the drop of a hat, lifting the boys to school, and just being there when needed.

7

Chapter 7

Brothers

Lauren

The boys were very different and yet similar.

Ryan had a huge personality and a mischievous side to him. He was a joker but had such a fighting spirit.

He would have been quite happy as an only child and loved teasing Matthew, who looked up to and adored him.

They got to a point where they were both the exact size, which I loved as I could dress them the same, which led a lot of strangers to think they were twins. I kept saying I was going to make the boys signs that said, "*We are not twins*", and the other sign would say, "*What the fuck are you staring at?*"

In hindsight, people thinking they were twins was partly my fault, considering they were the same size and dressed the same.

One day, while out, I was at the shops with the boys, the two of them in their pram; a lady was staring so hard that she tripped over a wet floor sign, and I shouted, "You see, you shouldn't be staring." I used to get so angry.

We tried three different prams with the boys. The first one was a side-by-side one, which didn't last too long as they kept irritating each other; correction… Ryan kept irritating Matthew. The second one was one behind each other, which worked well when Ryan sat in the front; otherwise, he would pull Matthews's hair. It wasn't the easiest to push, so we got a Phil & Ted one, which meant one child sat slightly above the other one, which worked well except for the one day when we went shopping.

We finished our shopping and walked to the car. A car pulled up and was waiting for our parking bay. I quickly took Ryan out of the front of the pram while Paul unpacked the grocery trolley. While I put Ryan's seat belt on, I looked out of the back window, and the next thing I saw was Paul trying to close the pram, but he was really battling with it, and I thought, *'Where's Matthew?'*

Yip, you guessed it, he was still in the back of the pram, as quiet as a mouse, and there was Paul, trying to fold down the pram. I don't know what the guy waiting for our parking bay must have thought.

Ryan loved sports and would love to play cricket when propped up against a couch. He used to play imaginary golf, and when he "hit" the ball, he would click his tongue like the noise it would make if you had hit a golf ball.

He loved to "walk" around; an adult would hold his hands, and he would be off; it was hard to stop once you started. Ryan loved telling secrets; he would make a rustling sound in your ear, which would be his secret. And he especially loved boxing with my aunt, Aunty Ba.

They would pretend to box each other, and one day, she boxed him, and he pretended to cry, but when she came near, he boxed her back.

He would pretend to cry a few times, and we would sing "Baby baby baby", and he would pack out laughing.

Ryan would always want to sit with the adults, and when we laughed, he laughed; he had such a wise soul.

Ryan would often volunteer Matthew for physio or blood tests, anything really that he didn't want to do; he would point and offer Matthew's services.

On the other hand, Matthew would not hurt a fly except for his weird obsession with hair.

He was such a gentleman and would often hold his hand out for a handshake, even to strangers, blowing them kisses or giving the biggest hugs.

He had lots of girlfriends and was the gentlest soul I'd ever met.

Matthew had also started riding at SARDA when he was three and absolutely loved riding his horse and his bike; he would sit on his knees like a little meerkat and bounce and squeak.

He loved animals, and Paul has already mentioned his relationship with our dog. One day, he irritated our cat and got too close, and she grabbed his face with her paws as if to say that's enough! Matthews' little face was priceless; he just stared at her in shock and then gave his nervous little laugh.

The boys started in separate bedrooms, but soon, we put them together and got a bunk bed. Ryan was at the top, and Matthew was at the bottom; having them together worked well as they shared clothes and toys.

Paul

Years on, I would get tattoos on my arms in remembrance of my precious boys; for Ryan, I have a Chinese symbol of a Tiger, representing Tiger, as in Tiger Woods for golf (the sporting side of Ryan) and, more importantly, representing his fight and tenacity. I have a Chinese symbol of innocence for Matthew, as that is what he was: an innocent, peaceful, and loving human. As Lauren said, they were so different in many ways but similar in others; these tattoos represented for me their dominant characteristic and what would live with me forever.

8

Chapter 8

Finally Meeting Our CS Family

Lauren

In 2009, a friend contacted me and said she was helping children with life-threatening illnesses by making some dreams come true. The boys would perhaps be interested in going in a racing car. I mean, which little boy wouldn't? So, my two tiny little boys each got a turn to be a part of Race to Live and rode in a race car around the track.

Ryan loved it and, when it was finished, had the biggest smile on his face, but Matthew wasn't that excited about it. He didn't cry but was happy to be out of the car.

The boys also did their first Argus cycling race that year. Ryan went on his little black scooter, and Matthew went in his push trike, and we pushed him. They came home with medals and beaming smiles on their faces. They may have been small and had huge challenges, but we were determined to treat our boys as we would any child and expose them to as much as possible.

That year, Jayne from *Amy and Friends* came back to me saying they would sponsor all four of us to go to the UK for the next retreat.

I was so excited; finally, I would meet other children like my boys and parents who were going through the same daily struggles as me. I had been chatting to a few moms via Facebook and following the website news, so it would be amazing to meet some of them finally.

We had lots to prepare; the boys needed passports, and we had to get visas for the UK. Closer to the time, we would have to organise enough medication and milk feeds to take with us as we didn't know what they had there.

The conference was only going to be four days long, and London was so far away so we arranged to stay with friends for a few days before the start of the event.

This was going to be our first long flight with the boys.

Finally, the day arrived, and we were super anxious; there was so much we had to remember to take. We would have to feed the boys on the plane, but we weren't allowed to take fluids on the plane, so we had to get a written letter from our doctor giving us permission.

Luckily, we had a row of four, so we didn't have anyone with us. The boys were actually really well-behaved and slept nicely on the plane. Once we were all settled, we started their feeds, very aware of other passengers watching.

Paul and I watched a movie each and then decided it was time to try to get some sleep. I think the anxiety of the last few days had finally kicked in, and I was feeling very tired.

Thankfully, the pumps didn't play up, and there was no vomiting, so all in all, it was a good flight despite trying to change a nappy in those tiny bathrooms.

We landed and looked forward to a few days with our friends before heading to the conference. I didn't realise at the time that this trip would change my life forever.

Spending time with our friends was so lovely, and we did all the touristy things and realised how lucky we are in South Africa to have private transport. It was not easy with a double pram and two disabled children.

The day before the conference started, we caught a train from London to Manchester, where someone would pick us up and take us to the hotel.

The train trip was lovely; it allowed us to see the countryside and relax a little after a very busy few days in London. We would be one of the first families to arrive for the conference, allowing us to settle in before the locals arrived. I couldn't believe how nervous I was. I had never seen another CS child before, well, not in real life anyway, and here we were, a long way from home. I felt very emotional and overwhelmed.

I walked into the hotel, almost holding my breath, and the friendliest people greeted us.

We were given a goodie bag, including *Amy and Friends* t-shirts, the itinerary for the next few days, an *Amy and Friends* CD, a Cockayne Syndrome pamphlet, and a few other things.

We walked around the corner, and there was Jayne. I had only ever spoken to her via Facebook, and now here I was, face-to-face with her in the UK. I knew straight away she was such a special person. After we exchanged huge hugs, she introduced me to her family, and then I met Amy, my first CS child. I had only ever seen photos, and it's hard to tell size from photos. She was much bigger than the boys but definitely not the usual size of a teenager, and she could talk and walk. I felt there was hope for my boys!

We sat and chatted for ages, and all her children were lovely. Amy was the oldest, then Jonathon, Ben, and Laura. Her children took a liking to my boys, so we didn't see much of them at the conference. The boys were always on one of the older kids' hips or being wheeled around. Every time we looked for them, they were with someone new, but it was okay because I knew it was safe and everyone there loved them. Our boys were like royalty, being carried around everywhere and in their element. They were having the best time with their friends.

I remember Jayne's kids saying the boys must have type 4 because they looked so healthy, which made me smile.

Slowly, other families started arriving, mainly from the UK, and it was like I was meeting celebrities. I had seen the children's faces on the website for so long that it felt surreal to see them in the flesh finally.

I met a little girl named Terri from Carlisle, Cumbria. She was the youngest of three children. Terri was the same age and size as Ryan but had type 1, like Amy so that she could walk and talk, although I found it difficult to understand what she was saying because of her accent. Then I met Thomas, who was in between my boys in age. Thomas was from Oxfordshire and had an older sister, Ellie. I fell in love with the little guy straight away. He had the same big personality as Ryan. Amazingly, when Thomas and Ryan saw each other for the first time, it was like they were long-lost brothers; they ran into each other's arms and hugged one another. It was the most beautiful thing I have ever witnessed. My heart sang when I saw that, and as a mom, I knew I had made the best decision to bring my boys here. From that moment on, they were best friends. My heart was happy. Ryan had found someone just like him.

They got up to lots of mischief together, like when someone brought a balloon, and the two of them decided they were not going to share it with anyone. When they had the balloon, they would bonk whoever came past them on the head, causing all the children to squeal with delight. I met Megan, Leo, and Taylor-Louise, who are all from the UK, too. They also had type 2, so they were smaller than my boys but spent most of their time in people's arms or in their buggies.

We met Josie, who was type 1 and also from the UK. She was adopted by Gill and Alan. There was Katherine, who also had type 1. Her parents were Susie and Charles, and I spent a lot of time with them, too.

I met June from Spain and a couple from Australia, Karen and Marc. Their daughter, Lauren, had passed away eight months before, but they still wanted to come to the retreat to celebrate and remember their daughter's life. They had taken some time off and were doing some travelling.

They were so lovely, and we spent a lot of time with them. After we met them, I told Paul how brave they were and that I would never return if our boys passed away. They were an inspiration to me and, I'm sure, to many others.

We met Eric and his mom, Ana, from America, and Nick and his mom, Jennifer, from Texas. They were all the same age as Amy (18 years old). Nick was Amy's boyfriend, and boy, did they love each other. On the last night we had a party and Nick "proposed" to Amy, it was so sweet. He gave her a ring, which she proudly showed off to anyone who wanted to see it. The plan was that they would get "married" at the next year's retreat.

The retreat was amazing. I can't give it justice here in words. I finally felt so at home. All the daily struggles we thought we were fighting alone seemed to disappear when we realised other parents were fighting the same battles.

We could feed our boys, and no one would stop and stare and ask questions. I stayed up late nearly every night chatting to the moms, but mainly to Cath, Thomas' mom. We each had a chance to go and speak to the doctors, and I was surprised when I realised our medical care was better than what most of the families were getting; this was because, in South Africa, we pay for private medical aid, whereas over there they have to wait months for appointments and equipment and they never see the same doctor. I felt very grateful for our medical team. The families there, however, were getting extra things paid for, like the feeds and nappies, and some of them were even given cars and could renovate their houses to accommodate their child's needs.

On the last day, we had a little service to remember the children who had passed away and to pray for all the other CS children, and I remember watching Karen and Marc and feeling utterly heartbroken for them. The siblings could go up and light a candle for the children if they wanted to, so when Jonathon (aged 10) went up, I thought nothing of it until he announced that he was lighting a candle for Ryan and Matthew from South Africa.

What? Did he just say that he is lighting a candle for Ryan and Matthew?

My heart stopped, and I was struck with such emotion. My eyes filled up, and my chest actually physically hurt. I was in such awe of this young boy who didn't even know us, yet he had taken us into his heart. What a massive toll it must be on the healthy siblings.

After exchanging details with everyone, we had to say goodbye, which was really hard as I knew we were going back home to no one who truly felt our situation, but at least now I had a new family, one that understood us deeply. I must admit, leaving was hard as I felt like I could have stayed there forever.

We gave Jayne and her family our South African thank you presents and Amy a teddy with a photo of Ryan and Matthew printed on it, said our goodbyes and promised to try and be back for the next retreat.

Once home, it was exciting to tell our families about who we had met and what we had learnt, but I also realised I felt strangely alienated and alone. Thank goodness for emails and Facebook. I could keep in touch with my new family, and I secretly hoped we would meet again soon. In the first week back, Amy and their friends had already started planning the next retreat and, of course, the wedding!

Paul

Whilst the retreat was amazing, it was hard for me. Without a doubt, I had created a bubble for myself and moved on with life without focusing on reality. I was constantly looking for the positive and clutching onto every little ray of light I found. But the retreat, for me, was too real. Lauren found meaning and a family of people to speak to, and that appealed to her personality trait of wanting to know the finer details and explore. For me, it was a reality check. I felt overwhelmed when talking to the parents who had lost kids. I also struggled to grasp the various hardships that emerged during the different points of the syndrome, and there were kids at all different stages. One real positive was meeting the other dads and seeing how Ryan bonded with the children, especially Tom. But to be honest, I was happy to leave. I had ticked the box, seen and heard what I needed to, and it was time to jump firmly with both feet back into my little safe bubble.

Lauren

My life had changed so much since the retreat, and my CS medical knowledge was growing. I stayed in touch with all the doctors: Dr Kang, Dr Neilan (who had diagnosed the boys) and Dr Laugel from Strasbourg.

These doctors were trying their best to find a cure and just some answers about CS.

Dr Laugel contacted me a few months later to say they were going to be doing a research study, and we would be part of it. Wow! Absolutely! A chance to help the doctors and other children with CS? Definitely!

They would sponsor all of us to go over even though they only needed us for two days of testing. We managed to wangle the dates around the next retreat. I was over the moon, but it also meant lots of admin as the testing would take place in Strasbourg, so this time, we would need both a French and a UK visa.

The French embassy was not very friendly, and our appointment was quite nerve-wracking. They needed loads of documents in a specific order, which ours weren't, so we were promptly sent out of the room and could only return once we had everything in the correct order.

We had left a question blank as we weren't sure if it meant where we came in from or where we landed. When she saw it blank, she asked where did you land, which we told her, and she answered, "OOhhhh, the difficult question"!

She really was not friendly at all.

We decided to stay an extra two days in Paris, do some sightseeing, and take the boys to Euro Disney. Then, we would fly over to London and attend the wedding of the year. Our flights were paid for, so it was just accommodation in Paris and spending money we had to budget for. We would stay a few days before the retreat in London in Susie's (Katherine's mom) apartment and do some sightseeing in London again. The whole trip seemed to be too good to be true. To make it even more special, all the CS children were going to be page boys and flower girls for the wedding, so I had some shopping to do. The boys needed to wear white shirts and black pants, and Jayne would organise the ties.

I was so touched, as this would probably be the only time my boys would be asked to do something like this.

I started buying many little South African gifts as I now knew more people. Amarula chocolates, biltong, African coasters, beaded animals. I bought Thomas a shirt that said, *"Someone who loves me bought me this shirt in Cape Town."* anything with butterflies on it as butterflies were a symbol for the CS children who had passed away. The butterfly symbolises rebirth. When the caterpillar becomes weary, it changes into a butterfly.

I was beyond excited to see everyone again and meet new families, but there was also a painful reality I had to deal with. Some of the beautiful CS children I had met the year before had passed away. I kept myself and my mind busy.

Packing to go away with the boys was a huge task. I had to remember absolutely everything. A few weeks before the flight, I started writing a list, and every day would remember something else that had to be added. We had to get medicine scripts beforehand as we didn't know what we could get over there as the laws in the UK were different from those in SA. We had to get doctor's letters allowing us to take certain medications and permission to allow us to feed the boys on the plane again.

I had to take their daily meds plus any other medication I thought we might need, like for pain, sleep, coughs, colds, and temperatures. We had to take enough milk, tubes and syringes, extra mickeys, plugs and nappies. We decided the best way to get around with the boys would be their double pram and not take walkers or buggies for them.

We got our visas almost hassle-free. The boys were required to do fingerprints, but because their little hands were quite stiff, it turned out to be quite a challenge, and the biometrics machine wouldn't read them, so we had to get special permission not to do it. The visas arrived, and we were good to go.

We had loads of luggage, so we decided every piece of luggage had to be on wheels for easier transport. It was an immensely exciting time. I think more for me, as the boys didn't know what was happening. Not only was I going to see my CS family again, but my boys were going to be page boys in a wedding, and we were going to Euro Disney!

Paul

I was a little less excited about the trip than Lauren. I was sold by the fact that we could also make the stay into a holiday, and we would spend some time in Paris (it would be my first time), go to Euro Disney and see great friends of ours in Amsterdam. I knew how important it was to support Lauren, as this was extremely important for her and the boys. I kept my optimism wrapped around me.

Lauren

We flew into Amsterdam and had a few hours wait there, so a friend picked us up, and we spent the day with them, walking around Amsterdam and seeing their home and their new baby.

Then we flew to Strasbourg, and a chauffeur picked us up.

We got to our hotel room quite late in the afternoon, so we decided to have a quiet evening as the next day, we were to be fetched early to be taken to the hospital. The boys had been so good, but they were starting to get a bit restless, so we knew we needed to have a quiet night as we didn't know what the next day entailed.

We were dropped at the entrance and given some broken English directions for where to find our Prof. Needless to say, we got lost, and no one in the hospital knew what or who we were looking for as we pronounced his name differently to how they say it. Eventually, I wrote the Prof's name down and asked someone, and we found him. We didn't know what to expect, but we completely trusted the Prof and liked him, so we weren't too concerned. He was young, about our age, and he spoke English very well, so he was easy to talk to.

They did blood tests, hearing tests, weight, height, and a general check-up with the boys.

Prof Laugel asked us if we would like to be tested for the gene for future children, and we both looked at each other and thought, *'I don't think there will be any more children, but we are here, so let's do it'.*

It was a very long day at the hospital, and by the end, we were all ratty and tired, but considering our time would help others, and that they had paid for us to be there, it was worth it.

Paul

We got to spend some time in the gardens and next to the river in Strasbourg, which was extremely memorable. I can remember playing rolly-polly with Ryan on the banks of the river with the backdrop of the spectacularly beautiful town of Strasbourg. Special times and memories. We needed that after the tough day we had had at the hospital, with the vast language barrier and all the technical conversations. Strausberg will always go down in my memory as one of the most beautiful cities I have had the pleasure of visiting. The challenge was the lack of English - understood and spoken, making it a very difficult city to navigate. This was a special time for us, though. We felt that having all the tests done would help families in the future understand more about this syndrome. Therefore, we felt we were really giving something back and hopefully making a difference to many families in the future.

Lauren

The next day, we were up early to find our way to the train station. Finding it was easier than we thought, but when we arrived, we realised the French do not like to speak English, so I had to ask them in my broken basic Afrikaans for tickets to Paris. They clearly preferred non-English speakers because we got our tickets with no problem after that.

We caught the train to Paris, which was amazing. The scenery was stunning, and it was so nice to sit and take it all in.

We then took a taxi to our hotel room. Because our time was limited, we had to try to fit in as much as possible.

We caught the hop-on-hop-off bus to see most of Paris and stopped and had a croissant and hot chocolate at one of the little pastry restaurants.

On the second day, we decided to tackle the Eiffel Tower with a double pram and two disabled children, which was not an easy task.

The queues weren't too bad, plus we, as South Africans, are used to queuing for everything.

We were in the queue, and a little boy standing next to us said to his mom, "Mommy, that boy has got crazy hair." He clearly didn't know we were English, so I said, "Yes, isn't it crazy?". He got such a fright that I was English and felt so embarrassed!

We made it up to the top of the Eiffel Tower after waiting in the queue for 45 minutes, but it was not easy. They do not allow prams past a certain point, so we had to carry the boys.

Paris was not easy with two disabled children, so our nights were spent in the hotel room with takeaways, a sin I know, but the boys needed to be tube-fed, and I didn't feel like stares from strangers.

Our last day in Paris was early; we caught the train to Euro Disney, and I don't know who was more excited.

We got there, and it honestly felt like I was in a dream. I felt like a child. The colours, the castle, the characters, it was just unbelievable.

Our boys were old enough for some of the rides, but getting them on was a fight as they were so small in size.

We managed to do many kiddie rides, and Paul went on a few adult rides.

It was a blisteringly hot day, one of the hottest Paris had had in years, which obviously was not good for our boys, so we had to try and keep them cool often.

They loved the parades and all the different things to see, and we managed to see so much, considering how hot it was and how little our boys were.

We got the last train back to our hotel and were all finished from a very busy day out. Finished but happy.

London was next, and we loved Susie's flat, which was so well-situated and easy to get to.

Paul

I loved Paris, or at least the idea of Paris excited me. I was not to be disappointed and have since had the opportunity to visit the city again a couple of times. As Lauren has said, it was not easy to tour the city with a double pram. I found it magical and romantic, and the energy there was almost charismatic. I was starting to realise I really enjoyed big cities and was slowly ticking them off after having the fortune of visiting London, Sydney, Singapore, Bangkok and Paris - just New York and Hong Kong to go on my immediate big city list. Naturally, France was also the home of the Tour de France, and whilst I was not yet an avid cyclist (still to come), I had been as a kid and had watched the tour circumvent the French region many times. The home of this event made it that much more special, never mind the history of rugby and tennis. I loved the coffee shops, learning the expensive mistakes of sitting at the window on the Champs-Élysées. A lesson in doing some research before you rush off somewhere: it's not always good to do things on a whim or off the cuff, which is typical of me.

Disney was also awesome. The train trip was a great way to get there, although the changing of trains was both nerve-wracking and difficult with the double pram, knowing if you got the change wrong or missed the next train, it meant a long wait or a huge delay, and we were in the middle of nowhere. Nevertheless, we got there in one piece with no drama and got to experience the beauty of the French countryside.

I was like a kid, like most guys. I had always enjoyed theme parks and had always been somewhat of an adrenaline junkie. My dad often reminds me of the story of when I was 2 or 3, just running blindly into the sea, with him having to pull me out only for me to do it over and over again. So, the idea of Disney was just fantastic. In all honesty, whilst it was a great day, it was also difficult, physically and emotionally. Physically, it was extremely hot and humid, so it was tiring, but emotionally, it was just as draining because the boys were not permitted on so many of the rides. I desperately wanted them to experience what I was, the exhilaration of the rides and thrills, especially Ryan. They certainly got to enjoy some rides and loved the experience, which is all that counted at the end of the day… in hindsight, it is a lesson of context and not projecting and expecting that your reality or what you enjoy is necessarily someone else's. So many lessons from these two most beautiful boys; we were very blessed!

Time to head to Manchester and for me to face the conference. I knew my role was supporting Lauren, so I needed to man up and face reality. I have a lot to thank Lauren for, as I have no doubt it is through these personal hurdles that I grew immensely, both in strength and, more importantly, in humility and appreciation of others.

Lauren

Arriving at the retreat, I felt, *Yes, I'm home.* Seeing all my friends and the kiddies was heart-warming. I just knew it was going to be even bigger and better for me than the first one.

There was huge excitement around the wedding, and people were coming from all over London, Amsterdam, Germany, Japan, and America. Ryan was so happy to see his friend Tom again, and Matthew, being Matthew, had all his girlfriends wrapped around his little finger.

As usual, I didn't see the boys as they were off playing with their friends and being passed around saying hi to everyone.

We all had our South African t-shirts on, and someone approached me and asked where Ryan's twin was.

She meant Thomas. They did look so alike.

The day of the wedding came, and there was a buzz of excitement among the children and the adults. Everyone went to their rooms to get ready, and I couldn't wait to see how beautiful my boys would look in their jeans, white shirts and pink ties.

People started coming downstairs slowly, and the children all looked beautiful. There were cameras everywhere you looked, and all the kiddies had the biggest smiles on their little faces.

Amy arrived on a luggage bag trolley that had been decorated with flowers; it was beyond special. She was glowing with pride.

The little ceremony was beautiful, and I don't think there was a dry eye in the room. The bride and groom were beaming, and their love for each other was so true and unconditional.

That evening was a huge celebration, with lots of dancing, singing, and smiling faces.

It was a truly special day for everyone who was lucky enough to be there.

For most of the CS children, it would be the only wedding they would be involved in, and all of them were so excited to be a part of the magical occasion. That evening, I stayed up the whole night chatting to the moms, and Paul took the boys to bed. We had an early lift in the morning, so I wanted to make the most of my time there.

We laughed, cried, and chatted, with people coming and going all through the night.

In the morning, one of the dads came through, and a feeding pump alarm was going off, and he said, "God, how I miss that sound," it was such a huge statement to make.

Our feeding pump goes off all the time, and it drives us crazy, and we scream and curse it daily, but there was a dad who had lost his daughter saying how much he missed that very annoying noise. It put everything into perspective again, and reality hit me.

I was very fond of this dad, who, unlike many men, was easy to talk to about Cockayne Syndrome. We spent a lot of time chatting, and I looked forward to our conversations because they were so real. The conference gave many people a safe space to talk without judgment.

Now, while the conference was focused on the CS kiddies and the doctors were there to chat with the parents, there were also other very important people there — the siblings. These children have a very hard life, as parents are often focused on their "sick" child only because they need more care and more of the parent's time. There are lots of CS siblings, and at the retreat, they get to be all together to chat if they want to or just to be with other siblings going through similar stuff. These kiddies take on so much: the anxiety of losing their brother/ sister, the sadness of watching their sibling deteriorate and the helplessness in their inability to do anything about the situation.

Then comes another stress: Are they carriers?

In the UK, they can only be tested when they are 16; some want to know, some don't.

Some worry they are carriers, and some worry they aren't and why their sibling had to get CS and not them; these are all real fears for them. The siblings are the silent sufferers, and they are true superheroes!!

Paul

The conference for me was, as I said earlier, difficult, but looking back, I realise I was not alone in my thinking. Most of the guys stuck together, speaking little of our kids and their challenges, but rather of sporting rivalries, which I guess was our way of dealing with it, all the time knowing it was good to be in the company of guys that were going through similar challenges (if you have seen Defending the Caveman - a theatrical show in South Africa, you will recognize this trait of a man). Some were dealing with the loss of their kids, others were dealing with the news of the diagnosis and what was to come, and many of us were in the throws of it and juggling work, friends, relationships, and the needs of our kids. The highlight for me was the Dad's Night when we went go-carting. It was great fun, burning off some emotional steam with a good few beers afterwards. It is amazing how people come together. We were all from different countries, financial positions and family circumstances, yet there was an understanding, respect, and brotherhood ... but it was still difficult. I never quite felt at ease. It was a wonderful conference, especially with the wedding, a remarkable and precious ceremony, definitely one that will outlast the sands of time!

9

Chapter 9

Big Decisions

Lauren

(January 2010 – December 2010)

Being a woman, I always knew I wanted to be a Mom, so obviously, when my two boys were born, I felt very fulfilled, and I felt I had found my purpose, BUT when they were diagnosed, I had a panic attack. If CS were going to rob me of my boys, I would have no children, and this thought was just too much for me.

I wanted to be able to think I would always be a mother, but after being at the retreats and witnessing how some kids don't come back the next year, I knew in my heart that I was probably going to lose my boys.

So, after many discussions and chatting with some moms, we decided we wanted to have another baby, but it scared us as although we loved our boys and would not have changed anything, we wanted a healthy child, which could not be guaranteed. For every pregnancy that Paul and I had together, there was a 1 in 4 chance of the baby having CS. Now, those odds don't sound too bad; that means there is a 3 in 1 chance that the baby would be healthy, but considering it had happened twice before, we really weren't sure what to do.

We eventually decided the best option for us would be a sperm donor.

It would be easier and cheaper than using an egg donor, and to guarantee that both of us didn't pass down the gene, we had to cut one of us out of the equation.

We met with the doctor at the fertility clinic, and after giving her all our history and discussing options, she sent us to chat with the psychologist. I suppose they need to ensure we are really sure before giving the go-ahead. After another discussion with the doctor, we returned and chose a donor.

What a strange process. There is no photo, just details on their appearance and some background on them, like interests and hobbies.

We joked and said we wanted the guy with olive skin because we were so pale or the guy with blue eyes because we wanted our baby to have blue eyes.

We eventually chose our guy, the one that sounded the most similar to Paul and in February, I had my first artificial insemination.

Because I fell pregnant so quickly with my boys, I thought the same would happen. This was not the case. We had three procedures in three months, and nothing happened. I then had a little op to make sure everything was ok. It seemed everything was in working order, but my eggs were apparently old. Seriously? I was only 34. Everyone I told laughed and had never heard that before.

I went on to more hormone treatments and medication to help me become pregnant. It became a total obsession and started taking over my life.

I would inject myself in my stomach on certain days to help with the insemination. It was a life change: keeping track of my hormones and my periods, changing my diet, being as healthy as possible, and not drinking alcohol. A year and seven artificial inseminations later, and still nothing happened. I was beyond disappointed. It became a serious emotional roller coaster ride. We spent a small fortune financially. Why wasn't it working?

I had had no problems before. I was heartbroken. Absolutely heartbroken after everything we had been through. Our options were reduced, and I didn't quite know what we would do next. That December, we went away with good friends and tried to switch off from all that had been happening and the decisions that lay ahead. Ryan was super miserable that holiday, which was very unlike him. He moaned a lot and was very restless; he only wanted to be cuddled, nothing else. So when we got back, I took him to the doctor.

Paul

Lauren was desperate to have another child, which naturally I supported. As Lauren said, we spent a small fortune trying to make this happen whilst mitigating the risks we faced in having a biological 3rd child. This felt strange, but I was good with it. By the time we realized it just wasn't going to happen, we started to discuss the alternatives.

Adoption seemed the only other way. I was not crazy about this idea. On the one hand, I knew I was giving a home and a family to a child. On the other hand, would I ever completely accept him/her as my own? I knew it was important for Lauren and agreed to consider and investigate it. It was quite a process. I will never forget that day waiting at the adoption agency, sitting with Lauren, just knowing and realising fully for the first time that I could simply not do this. I was going to break my wife's heart, and how could I do this after all she and I had been through already? But to have a happy household, we both needed to be happy. It was one of the most difficult discussions we had had, and I could see the disbelief and disappointment in her eyes whilst she tried to assure me she understood. I felt like a weight had been lifted off my shoulders, no wait… the whole world had been lifted off my shoulders.

After many discussions and debates, we finally came to the conclusion that we had been blessed to have two children in our lives and that a 3rd was not going to happen, so I booked in to have a vasectomy done. All was set. Just before I left, I asked the surgeon what the recovery time was; he asked why. I told him I was going on a skiing trip in 5 weeks' time and I didn't want to be in any discomfort. He said I should be fine but suggested we wait until I returned just to be sure. I agreed with this advice. This was a boys' ski trip. I was going with my best mate and a couple of other friends and meeting one of my other best mates from Amsterdam over in Austria. I couldn't contain myself, and I couldn't risk it. This turned out to be a great decision; little did I know.

Lauren

On 8 January, we were admitted as Ryan had sepsis around his Mickey, so Prof Brown removed it and replaced it with a new one.

While he was under, they noticed he was a bit oedematous (holding water), and his blood pressure was 120/70.

They did a urine dipstick and discovered that his urine was 3 + protein, but his blood chemistry was normal, so Ryan was put on antibiotics.

A week later, we had a check-up with Deon, and he decided to check Ryan's BP again.

We went down to the paed ward and did the test. When we showed the result to Deon, he just shook his head and said that they had done it wrong and they must repeat it. We did the test three times. Deon even used Ryan's arms and legs the final time, but the result remained unchanged.

I will never ever forget his face. Deon is a calm guy, but when he saw the reading, I knew something was very wrong. Ryan's blood pressure was 160/120. He raced back to the room, and I could hardly keep up. With Ryan in my arms. He shut the door, leaving me in the waiting room; I tried not to panic.

Deon phoned Priya Gadjar, head of Nephrology at the Red Cross Children's Hospital. He came out after a few minutes and called me into his room. He told me that with Ryan's reading, my son should be in a coma. Now, I panicked. We were admitted straight away. I phoned work to tell them that I wasn't coming back and phoned Paul in tears and told him to come straight to the hospital.

And so our year started on a very scary note. Ryan had high blood pressure, but what exactly did that mean?

After chatting with Karen Fieggan and Prof Laugel, it was agreed that we should do a whole lot of other blood tests and a renal ultrasound. We found out his kidneys weren't functioning as well as they should be, but we didn't know if the kidneys had caused the high BP or if it was the other way around. So Ryan was started on amlodipine and Pharmapress straight away to try to get his BP down. We were in the hospital for a few days, and when it seemed as though we were on top of things, we went home, but that didn't last, as Ryan just wasn't well. January was our highest admissions, and I think it was about ten for the month.

It was also suggested we go to the Red Cross again for assistance and a renal biopsy as the hypertension was proving to be very resistant to treatment. The cause of the hypertension/kidney problem was one anxiety; the other was the very real danger of a stroke or cardiac failure from this exceedingly high BP for such a small boy. A sustained BP of 160/120 is a high risk for an adult, so you can imagine what it meant for Ryan.

For the next few months, we were managed at the Red Cross with occasional checks at the Medi-Clinic.

While the Red Cross has the most amazing doctors and staff, the hours spent waiting for appointments got to be too much, so we decided to see a private doctor with regard to Ryan's kidney function. Our paed did not approve, but we had to do what we felt was best for our boy.

In February, we were admitted for a chest infection, vomiting and lethargy again in March. All the blood tests were repeated, and Ryan was put on more meds for his kidneys.

So, at this point, he was on Amlodipine, Enalapril, Losec and Ciprobay, and they had discovered that he had high cholesterol, too. (Quite a cocktail of drugs/medication for anyone, let alone a child).

It had been such a rough start to the year that the days just blurred painfully into each other. Paul and I felt like we were passing ships in the night, as we both dealt with the hospital stress differently.

I started feeling extremely tired, run down and just plain horrible. I put it down to the stress but eventually decided there must be something really wrong with me, so I decided to go see my doctor. On the morning of my appointment, I told my staff I was going to the doctor, and my one teacher asked me if perhaps I was pregnant. I laughed at the comment and then thought, '*Shit, when last did I have my period?*'

Now, if you remember, I had been on fertility until December, and January had started with such a bang that I hadn't given birth control another thought until now. I went to the doctor, and she examined me and asked me the same thing.

She checked my urine and sent me for blood tests, a pregnancy test included. I got home and phoned Paul to tell him about my appointment and mentioned to him that the doctor was checking to see if I was pregnant, too.

He sounded pretty shocked; I mean, I was too, but there was a little part of me that was super excited, too. The rest of that day seemed extremely long, and eventually, the doctor phoned to say I was nearly 8 weeks pregnant. I think I went through every emotion in the space of a few minutes. I was happy, excited, anxious, and scared, and my head felt like it was going to burst with all the conflicting feelings. I could not believe it; I am Miss Organised. I don't get surprised. I plan everything. Wow, could this really be happening?

I was totally freaking out. How was I going to tell Paul? Was he going to blame me somehow?

I told him the doctor had phoned and that I was pregnant; he was completely shocked but handled it well.

After I phoned Paul, I went down to the pharmacy and got some pregnancy multivitamins. I was so bad with taking tablets, but through all my pregnancies, I always took vitamins.

Paul

That call I got from Lauren I will never forget. I was in a meeting at the time. She called until I picked up. When she gave me the news, I was in complete disbelief. I had so many emotions; thinking about the fact I had planned to have the snip, and now Lauren was pregnant could be a sign of good things. I don't believe in things happening for a reason. Rather, things happen, and you deal with them, whatever they are (good or bad). But, on this occasion, I allowed myself to think just this ... but boy, was I anxious about the whole thing, excited but anxious. I mean, let's be honest: if we had to go through this all again, would we actually make it through the 3rd round? BUT, if it didn't, and we had a healthy boy, wouldn't that be the most amazing and special blessing we could ever receive!!!

I knew it was not going to be an easy path ahead in the next 8 or so months, but my optimism soon enveloped me, and I couldn't help thinking of the possibilities.

Lauren

I started to get really excited about the possibility of having a healthy baby, but then I also panicked about the baby having CS. That night, I went to my mom's for dinner as it was her boyfriend's birthday, and I told her and my sister. Although we wanted to jump for joy, there was also a part of us that was anxious.

That night, when Paul got home, I hugged him tight and joked with him I thought he might not come home. He laughed and said, of course, he was coming home. This wasn't what we had planned. We never wanted to be put in this situation as we both felt differently about terminating, but we would take one day at a time and try not to stress in the meantime.

The next day, I phoned Karen Fieggan to ask her what we could do to test the baby and e-mailed the Professor to ask him for Paul and my mutation codes; it turned out we would need them after all. Friends phoned that week to see how I was feeling, and I told them I had third-child syndrome. It took some of them a while to figure it out.

We decided we would tell close friends and family but not work people and extended family.

Telling friends and family was interesting. Some of them were very concerned, and you could see they disapproved of the risk we had taken, and some were over the moon, convinced that this baby was going to be our healthy blessing. I felt that if we had to make some hard decisions, we would need the support.

Paul

I remember feeling quite irritated when we picked up peoples' concerns, only natural, of course, but I was like, *'This is our thing; we need your support, encouragement and positivity, not some awkward concern.'* I don't take negativity well; in fact, it drives me wild (mad), so I had to bite my tongue many times and, as they say, "smile and wave" ... whilst cursing under my breath.

Lauren

Emotions were all over the place; one moment, I would feel so excited; the next, really worried; all the 'what if' questions played in my head, and I still felt really terrible. A week after we found out, I went to my gynae for a check-up. It all felt so surreal, but when we saw our baby on the scan and heard the heartbeat, time stood still, and everything seemed perfect.

It was the battle of the emotions, so bittersweet. We wanted to be happy but were so worried, too. We decided we wouldn't find out the sex of the baby until after the tests came back, and then, only if everything was normal. We didn't want to make it harder for ourselves.

I still felt so nauseous, but eating small amounts helped, and I craved scrambled eggs with freshly cut-up tomatoes. In May, Ryan was again admitted for an infection around the mickey site, and the swab cultured MRSA, multi-drug resistant staph, pseudomonas, and klebsiella. These are all nasties, so we were treated with antibiotics and an IV. I had to tell Deon our news - which I did over the phone. He, too, was surprised.

I was pregnant and had to be careful with what I was exposed to, but my priority was still Ryan.

After being in contact with Karen and the Prof, it was decided that I would have a CVS (chorionic villus sampling) done. This was similar to an amnio but could be done earlier, and we wanted to make decisions as early as possible.

As no one had ever had CS testing in utero before in South Africa, we needed the professor's help. So at 11 weeks, I went in, Paul came with me, and the nerves were out of control. I lay on the bed shaking; in front of me was a screen. The doctor came in and started getting ready.

The biggest syringe I had ever seen was lying on the table, and I could see Paul was not looking comfortable. They switched the screen on, and there was our baby, our teeny tiny little baby, and then came the syringe. You could actually see the syringe penetrate my stomach and go in.

Paul

It is important to note two key things at this point: 1. Lauren and I were on polar opposite sides of thinking if the baby had any challenges in what we would do, and 2. I am completely needle-phobic, so seeing that needle for one was traumatic, and then seeing them stick it into my wife's stomach, where my unborn child was chilling, was just a completely new level. I almost felt sick, and nothing was happening to me -directly!

Lauren

The baby lay there quietly, not knowing what was going on until the syringe started jabbing and scraping the sides of the placenta, trying to get a sample and then all of a sudden, the baby started moving. I felt the baby's fear; it was terrible and quite a traumatic experience, but one that had to be done.

I was so relieved when it was finished and sent home to rest in bed for the next two days. Now, the waiting game started.

We were told the results would take two weeks, but after 15 days, they phoned to say they did not have an outcome yet.

Paul

This was like being stuck on 99 in a cricket match and not being able to get the ball off the square to get that 1 little run you needed; you are positive you can make it, but there is always a chance you won't.

Lauren

I had decided that that year I wouldn't go to the retreat as we didn't know what the results were going to be and how we were going to handle them, so I told Amy and friends we were unable to fly out to the retreat but told Jayne and Catherine the real reason. We still didn't want everyone to know.

We had decided we would have an early birthday party for Ryan in case the results were not what we wanted and we might not feel up to having a party, so we had a small party for our boy at the end of May.

Life carried on, and we focused on Ryan and his blood pressure. Then he got sick, and we landed back in hospital with chest problems. Paul and I started feeling sick, with flu-like symptoms, and just thought we had caught the same germs as Ryan.

Ryan's birthday arrived, and we were in the hospital. The staff were very sweet and organised a big cupcake for him. He had perked up a bit, and we were waiting for a sputum result. Ryan hated physio for his chest as much as he hated normal physio. He fought, screamed, and tried to vomit, but everyone knew his tactics, so he never got out of it.

I spent the day with him, and then my mom and sister were going to come in the late afternoon so Paul and I could have dinner together. I had just gotten home and was getting ready to jump into the shower when my phone rang; it was Karen. I thought she would tell me they still didn't have results.

I told her what a tough week we had had with Ryan, and he was in the hospital, and then she told me that they hadn't found the mutation. I was like, '*OK, so now what,*' and she said to me, "Lauren, the baby doesn't have it." I could not believe my ears. Was she really saying that our baby was healthy? I will never forget those 6 words. "Lauren, the baby doesn't have it."

I couldn't help myself; I burst into tears. I was in complete shock; what a miracle. All I could say in return as I sobbed down the phone was that if I were with her, I would give her a huge kiss and hug.

It's hard to explain how I felt in the moments after I stopped crying. I felt the lightest I had felt for years. I was shaking, literally shaking all over. I asked her if she knew the sex of the baby, and she didn't because we had decided not to know, so they had not kept a record of it. When our conversation finished, I put the phone down and just stared in the mirror with the biggest grin. My cheeks hurt; I was smiling so much.

I got into the shower with the biggest smile, and the tears flowed freely.

Paul arrived home just as I got out of the bathroom, and I ran to him, still crying. "Our baby is healthy; our baby is healthy!" I said as I held him. He was so happy, and we were both so relieved and so excited;

our dream of a healthy baby was about to come true. After four weeks of waiting for results, we got the best news ever on Ryan's 8th birthday.

Paul

We got the 100! Wow, how do you explain this or put this into words? What a moment! You constantly tell yourself everything is going to be alright (fake it until you make it - one of my favourite sayings), but to protect yourself; you allow yourself to believe there is a chance it may not go as planned, so the relief, the joy, the ecstasy was off the charts … the stress and pain had been worth it … this was a blessing. I had already decided I would have a tattoo that would symbolise something to do with blessing and completeness … this child, I had no doubt, would complete me and our family … bring it on! I was now super excited!!

Lauren

I started calling my family. My mom and sister were so excited they came to visit after the hospital, and we celebrated by eating chips and drinking hot chocolate. My phone did not stop; as word got around, family and friends sent messages and phoned to say how happy they were for us. The next day, I planned to phone my gynae so we could find out the sex.

I went to bed that night with a big smile on my face and woke up the next morning with it still there. I couldn't stop smiling. It felt so surreal. *Did last night really even happen*?

Our high was not to last long. The next day, Deon phoned to say that Ryan had been diagnosed with Swine Flu and that it was super dangerous for pregnant women. I felt my stomach tighten. There was a lump in my throat. I did not know what I was going to do. How was I going to carry on now? When he said that, my whole body stiffened; there was a huge knot in my stomach. This couldn't be happening. What were we going to do? Paul and I had flu-like symptoms as well.

Paul

This is not what I needed to hear; I was like, FFS, seriously? ... just get our hopes and dreams into place, and then you hit us with this ... come on! Cut us some slack here! I thought, '*Let us at least wallow in the joyful news we had received for a few days, even a week if you don't mind.*'

Lauren

We sent Matthew to his grandparents so he wouldn't get it, and Paul, Ryan and I had to go on Tami Flu. The problem was we didn't know the side effects on the baby, from a massive high to a nightmare.

I went to see a pulmonologist and the gynae to check on the baby, and thankfully, the baby seemed fine. It was a few days at home in quarantine, and we all slowly started feeling better, and Matthew could return home. It was nice to have everyone back under the same roof again.

As soon as I felt better, I was in full Lauren, aka Miss Organised, mode. I had a baby coming, and there was so much to do !!

First, to find out the sex, I phoned Aneen and again because we didn't want to know the sex, she did not write it down, so I would have to wait until my next appointment, which was only in a week's time.

I loved telling people I was pregnant; it was one of the best feelings in the world. Everyone we told had money on the baby being a girl; they figured a healthy baby, different pregnancy, must be a girl.

I couldn't imagine having a girl. I mean, I always wanted a girl because I grew up with a sister, but I was used to my boys; plus, if I had a girl, I would always be broke because the girls' clothes were so damn cute.

Finally, the day came, and we went to the Fetal Assessment Clinic, where they confirmed the baby was a boy.

I wasn't really surprised. I phoned my mom, and she was convinced I was lying. Now I could really start making things happen, first to plan the nursery!!

Paul

A healthy boy!

I could not help but let my fantasies take me away from time to time, thinking of the days ahead I could enjoy. These fantasies did come with a sense of guilt, though. What about Ryan and Matti? I needed not to cast them aside (not that would ever happen), but was it wrong to dream of these things when my first 2 born were not able to do these things?

10

Chapter 10

Family of Five

Lauren

We had gotten rid of everything as we wouldn't have another, so we had to start again. But this time, being the third, you know what you need and what you can live without! My pregnancy was very different to the other two; I felt horrible until about 18 weeks and yet couldn't stop eating. I remember going away with my mom and aunt and cousins, and my one cousin tried to keep up with my eating and felt so ill.

They called me the beast!! I contacted my dietician, and she suggested I drink a pregnancy shake, too, which I did. It was delicious and definitely helped me.

Paul and I realised that with the baby on the way; we really would need help with the boys and the house, so we decided it was time to find a full-time nanny, something we had never had before.

Where do you even start?

As I ran my own school, I came into contact with a lot of nannies, so word got out, and soon I had a few potential people.

We had had bad luck with nannies before, so we were hoping we would find the right person the first time.

Our last experiences included ladies sleeping on the couch when I was out, another one going through all my private things in my office drawer, and another one stealing a wallet from our local shop, and we had the police at our door.

We interviewed a lady, a friend of one of the nannies from my school, and she seemed lovely, so we started with her. Initially, she was really there for housework in the morning, and in the afternoon, she could take the boys for a walk. It was a very stressful pregnancy, though, as Ryan really wasn't well, and in September, we were called into Deon's office to discuss Ryan's end-of-life plan. I saw Karen Fieggan there for the first time since that wonderful phone call and gave her the biggest hug.

A week after our chat with Deon, our medical team, Deon, Doctor Billi, Michelle, and a palliative care nurse met us at our house, and we went through our end-of-life plan.

It felt so unreal, yet it was good to have a plan in place.

Paul

This is a process I can tell you no parent should go through; I haven't yet had to do this with my parents or a friend, which I imagine would also be very traumatic, but to do an end-of-life plan for your firstborn son at the age of 9 is just really hard, and a very big reality check (again, I seemed to have many of these moments).

Don't get me wrong, we were very aware of how ill Ryan was, and we were not in denial, but there's nothing quite like a process such as this to drive the graveness of the message home. Again, whilst I was very quiet through the discussion, I went into my very calm state, as I seem to do under extreme emotional pressure, absorbed it, and knew that every day from here on out would be a special day with Ryan. I also knew he was a fighter amongst fighters and would likely defy the odds.

Lauren

A few weeks later, Ryan was really struggling, so I phoned the doctors and was shocked to hear that they weren't going to do anything as that is what we had agreed on; it was a bitter pill to swallow, but I knew deep down there wasn't much more we could do for Ryan except keep him comfortable. We seemed to proceed through the plan quickly, and before we knew it, Ryan was on morphine 6 hourly. We moved him into our bed so he could be with us. He didn't like moving a lot and wasn't awake much. It was very special to be with our big boy when he was awake, but he got tired quickly, so we knew if he were awake for a bit, he would be finished the next day.

Life got quite tricky as we would need a babysitter just to go to the shop, and instead of going to the grandparents for dinner, they would come to us.

Now, people who know me know I love photos, so I contacted a friend and asked if he could take some family photos of us, as we weren't sure if Ryan would hang on until his brother came.

We went for photos, but Ryan wasn't well and wasn't awake much, but we managed to get a few good ones of the boys and my big tummy.

In October, we noticed Ryan would get a fright when we approached him, and one day, when he was awake, he just fell off our bed. We realised my big boy couldn't really see anymore.

Paul

It really just all seemed so cruel; we felt so helpless and wanted him to have peace, but it almost seemed he refused to give in despite his body giving up on him. He had so little sight, to know he had lost that little bit he had left, that he couldn't see us, was devastating. The confusion and scariness that must have caused him was a terrible cross to bear for Lauren and me. We knew, though, that he was fighting for a reason and was not giving up, and we needed to be there for him and give him our greatest love and support.

Lauren

I used to love getting into bed at night because Ryan would sleep cuddled up in my chest with his arm around my neck. When he did that, all I could feel was pure love. We would hold each other the whole night, despite some nights my arms getting pins and needles. This was such a special time for me and a memory I am so grateful for. While Ryan slept in my arms one night, I heard a "flapping" sound. I put the light on and noticed it was his eyelids were "flapping". I phoned Deon, and he said Ryan must be having a seizure. Fortunately, it was short but very scary.

A few weeks later, it happened again. We gave him medicine, which didn't seem to help, so we charged off to the hospital, but by the time we got there, it was over, so we went home. During those few weeks, we can't pinpoint exactly when we think Ryan must have had a stroke, as his one arm always seemed quite limp.

Paul

Things were getting very real. I am not sure anyone really knows how to deal with these situations, particularly when it is your child. You start going to bed, hoping it doesn't happen again. Ryan, as had become his mantra, was a fighter, my Tiger. He was not going down; no matter what life threw at him, he kept going, defying the odds time and time again. While this was an extremely difficult time, Ryan kept showing us how much fight he had and how much we all had to be grateful for and live for. He fought on and on, even at this stage, trapped in this painful and insulated life. There were times I thought, '*My little man, why not just give in? What's the point?*' but the point was clear: he had a brother to meet, a mom and dad and, of course, Matti, whom he loved and was not prepared to let go.

Lauren

The pregnancy was going well, but when I was just over 30 weeks, my gynae told me I had something called uterine notching, which usually causes high blood pressure. Luckily, I had low blood pressure, so it would be okay as long as it stayed low. With my history, however, they were not sure I would make full term and weren't going to chance it, so it was decided that they would perform a Caesar at about 37 weeks. With everything going on, we were still in discussions about our baby's name. I really loved the name Daniel, but Paul wasn't convinced, and then one of my teachers said to me if we named him James Ryan, he would be named after both his brothers. I loved that idea!!

We didn't tell anyone what we were thinking as A- we hadn't decided yet, and B- everyone always has an opinion on every name.

We were given a date, and all seemed to be okay, but a week before my Caesar, Ryan took a turn for the worse, and we thought he was in a coma. He wasn't really responding, so we had Doctor Billi and Deon come and check on him, and it was agreed that if anything happened with Ryan, we would postpone the Caesar until after the funeral.

I will never forget that day, 11 /11/2011.

The day before my Caesar, Ryan was much the same, so I phoned Deon to chat, and he had amazingly arranged a private nurse to be with Ryan while I was going to be in the hospital; all we had to do was sneak Ryan into the hospital when I arrived. Later that day, I was walking into the gym to take Matthew to his swimming lesson when I heard someone whistle for me. It was my Dad; he had surprised me and come down for the birth. I think everyone was feeling highly anxious and very emotional. My mom slept over that night to be with Matthew. She would get him ready for school the next day. That evening, I packed my bag and all the meds and things I needed for Ryan and the baby.

I had a disturbed night's sleep. My mind was racing the whole night. Thinking of little Matthew, who now wouldn't be the youngest and had no idea of what was about to happen. Thinking of Ryan and how he had fought so hard to still be with us and, of course, thinking of a new little one whom we would meet in the morning. What would he look like? Would he be healthy? I know the tests had come back negative for CS, but deep down, there was still that worry.

When I woke up, I felt calm. I showered and got everything together.

Said goodbye to my Mom and Matthew. The next time I would see him, he would be a big brother. I couldn't imagine him as a big brother; he was just so little with the most innocent personality.

We had borrowed a carrycot and very carefully put Ryan in it with his favourite blanket. We couldn't put him in a car seat as he really couldn't sit up anymore. He went in the back seat, and I sat next to him. I am still wondering today why on earth we didn't take the car seat out so I could have had a more comfortable drive to the hospital!!

I went to check myself in, and Paul snuck in with Ryan and took him to the paediatric ward. Once I had checked myself in, I went up to the paeds ward and saw Trudy, our favourite nurse, and she gave me the biggest hug. Emotions were running high for everyone. Deon told me the hospital felt desperately sad for me, and they had never had a situation like this before, where parents were welcoming a new baby only to say goodbye to another.

We got Ryan settled in, and when I left him, I felt exceptionally emotional. We went up to the maternity ward, and they came to fetch me as we arrived. I quickly went to the bathroom and then was wheeled off. The nerves started kicking in now; this was really happening. Our third Caesar, our second one, was not great, so hopefully, this one would be better. I was super anxious, not only for what was about to happen but also because we had such a close relationship with Deon, and now he was going to see me naked. How ridiculous!!

While we were in the theatre waiting room, Paul turned to me and said I think we should name him James Ryan. Paul, too, was overwhelmed with emotion. We went in, and Deon, Aneen, and the anaesthetist were there. I was given my spinal block and almost instantly couldn't feel my legs. Unlike the last Caesar, Paul decided to sit at the top next to my head. We chatted with Deon while Aneen did her thing and were quite calm. Then, there was some tugging and pulling, and Aneen announced the baby was ready to come out. The anaesthetist took our camera and started taking pics. Paul stood up and saw our beautiful boy come out with a "big" head. They had to use forceps to get him out as his head was bigger than the cut. Deon took him and weighed and cleaned him up. He was a whopping 3,4 kgs, the same size both his brothers were together. The baby cried, and we knew everything was ok. Deon wrapped him up and gave him to Paul, who then brought him to me. Our beautiful miracle, our healthy baby, was here. He was put on my chest, and I just stared at our precious angel with angel kisses on his eyelids, a red rash on each eyelid. I could not believe it; we had our third son, James Ryan Spagnoletti.

My face hurt from smiling so much, and my eyes were stinging, a combination of holding back tears and just pure emotional exhaustion.

We were still in the theatre when Deon's phone rang; Karen was phoning to find out if all was okay. I was wheeled into recovery, still with James on my chest; at what point was he going to be whisked away? But he wasn't. He stayed with me, and I even fed him before we got to our room, something I couldn't do with my other two boys. This was all new to me.

Paul phoned the grandparents and announced the safe arrival of James Ryan, and I think there were tears from everyone. It felt as though everyone had been holding their breath, but now that James had arrived and was healthy, everyone could breathe again.

As soon as we got to my private room, I wanted to know how Ryan was; even though I was ecstatic about welcoming my new baby, my priority was checking on Ryan. Unfortunately, he was very unhappy in the paeds ward, so I requested they bring him up to me, and I could see all the heartbroken looks on the nurses' faces. They put him in a single bed right next to mine, and I asked the nurses to take James for a bath. Although having James with me was amazing, I felt overwhelmed and needed time to check on Ryan. By the time he was back, the grandparents and Matthew had arrived, and everyone was so emotional. Well, except for Matthew, who had no idea what was going on.

Paul

It was funny how, in my first Caesar experience, I thought it was the most amazing thing ever, and I would stand in for dads not up to it, but by the 3rd, I was not handling the whole experience quite as well. Perhaps cutting through the scar tissue made it a less pleasant experience to be the bystander, but as Lauren said, emotions were off the charts for this birth. It felt like the hospital had reached a standstill for us that day; everyone walked on eggshells. I, myself, felt like I was breaking into a sweat walking into the operating theatre from all the anxiety and stress. It felt like 1000 degrees in there that morning.

That moment when James's head popped out and that little cry of his was one of my life's most beautiful sounds and moments, and it was completely overwhelming. What a true blessing. Life was complete; we had a healthy boy!!

I remember grabbing Matti and holding him in the air. He just squealed with joy, not because James had arrived but just because that is what this sweet, innocent, happy little boy did … his eyes were bright as buttons; life was good, except Ryan was not.

I gave James his first stuffed toy (which he still has today). It was a blue Smurf. I had bought it before he was born, and I had said my boy could be blue, but if he was healthy, that was all I wanted. This little blue Smurf, affectionately referred to as "Smurf-dog" (not sure why), symbolised a new hope and a different journey for us as a family.

But back to our reality, and I am not sure many have faced this, but here we were, on the one hand celebrating this amazing miracle and a newborn, and on the other, back in the ward, our first son was battling to survive and fighting for his life!! Having increasingly more and more fits, blind now, white as a ghost, deep-set eyes and crusty lips, sleeping most of the time with the odd moan to let you know he was still there, heavily dosed with morphine to subdue the pain, but he won't just let go … the ying and the yang … on steroids!

Lauren

We put James in the bed with his brothers and took some pics. Matthew was very intrigued by this new little person. That day and the next was a whirlwind of visitors and emotions. It was very difficult for me. I had a newborn who was extremely hungry, so I wanted to feed him every few minutes, and Ryan just wanted his Mommy. The first night was excruciating. I was feeding a lot and hearing Ryan moan, and I just couldn't handle it. I needed both my babies with me. So that night, I had Ryan in one arm and James in one arm. The nurse was lovely, but I was their Mom. It was not working, so I told Deon and Aneen I needed to be discharged early.

The constant flow of visitors continued at home, and meals came flooding in. Our house looked like a florist with all the flowers. Ryan was more settled now we were at home but was very tired from his hospital outing, so he slept a lot. I'm still not sure how I managed to do Ryan's feeds and meds and have a hungry newborn, plus Matthew, who just had to slot in.

The first few months were a bit of a blur as we settled into being a family of five.

I tried to breastfeed as much as I could but couldn't seem to keep up with the demand of hungry James, so I had to top him up with formula bottles. James slept in our room for the first few months, so I didn't have to get out of bed for feeds; only poor little Matthew had to sleep in his own room. My life consisted of little sleep, as Ryan slept in my arms, and I was up every four hours to feed James. When I got out of bed at 6:30, it felt like a whole day had passed already. I would get Matthew ready for school. James changed, dressed, and fed, and checked Ryan was okay. I would get dressed, check on my school, and ensure everyone arrived and was settled.

I would then go back inside, check on Ryan and give him his meds, get James to sleep, cook for school, do grocery shopping, do school admin, feed James, and check on Ryan and my school. The nanny would stay with Ryan, and sometimes James and I would go and fetch Matthew from his school. When we got home, the nanny would take Matthew for a walk, and I would be with Ryan and James and check on my school when needed. It was a very busy time, and I'm not quite sure how I functioned!

Paul

I must say, during this time and for a long time to this point, even when Ryan was well, it was a huge help having Lauren's mom more than most days taking the boys to school. I would drop them at her house on the way to work, and she would then take them to school. This helped in many ways. It helped Lauren and me from a time perspective, but I also still struggled with the school my boys had to go to, so not physically going was often easier, although I am super grateful for what they did and how they cared for my boys, just my "snobbiness" side coming out I guess. This especially helped when Ryan was so sick.

11

Chapter 11

Housebound But Making The Most Of It

Lauren

At about five months, we decided we wanted James christened but couldn't take Ryan out, so the minister who married us very kindly came to our house to do a service. James wore the same christening outfit that Ryan had worn, and it was a very special day celebrating our beautiful miracle boy!

We invited family and close friends and had a delicious brunch afterwards.

I took as many photos as possible with the three boys and decided another photo shoot was due, so we returned to my friend, who very kindly took some lovely photos of the boys, memories to treasure forever!

I can't even begin to tell you how happy I was with my arm full of boys; I loved having three children.

The next few months were very up and down, but we quickly got into our routine. Ryan was unhappy to be moved and was now sleeping most of the day. Every now and then, he would surprise us and be awake; we treasured that time so much.

Often, when the other two boys were down for the evening, we would go get Ryan, and he would lie on my chest in the lounge, and we would have our big boy to ourselves. But life was not easy. We couldn't take Ryan anywhere, so we had to rely on babysitters for everything, even just doing grocery shopping. Grandparents and my sister stepped in hugely and spent lots of time at our house.

Christmas was at our house so that Ryan could be with us without travelling anywhere.

It was a bittersweet Christmas, trying to be excited about celebrating James' first Christmas but having to check on my dying child in the room every few minutes.

That year, we had a small party for Ryan as he wasn't well. What do you buy a dying child?

My birthday was two weeks after Ryan's, and it was going to be my 35th, so I decided to have a big party (I do love my birthday, so any excuse to have a big party …).

I decided to have a dress-up party at home, organised snacks and drinks, and spent hours putting a music list together, but as the day got closer, I felt maybe I shouldn't be celebrating as my son was so ill.

Friends convinced me to go ahead, so James and Matthew slept out, and Ryan stayed at home in our bed.

Needless to say, all the stress and anxiety of the last few months took its toll, and I had too much to drink and was fast asleep by ten.

I was so disappointed the next day as I had spent hours preparing everything. The few hours I did make, though, were super fun, and it was great to see friends.

The next day, we stayed at home and spent the whole day playing with Matthew and James in the lounge. James was sitting on his little doughnut cushion, and Matthew was beside him. I took a sequence of photos, starting with Matthew slowly getting closer to James and James, very excited by this, to Matthew slowly grabbing James' ear and gently tugging. At this point, James still thought it was funny, but slowly, Matthew started to pull his ear a little bit harder, and the photos show James' face quickly changing from excitement to pain and then tears!

My real birthday came, and I had my mom, sister, and in-laws for dinner. Deon popped in with flowers, which was so kind of him.

To think 9 years ago, two weeks before my birthday, I had just become a Mom for the first time, floating high and only had happy thoughts of my future with my son, and now here I was with three beautiful boys, but my firstborn, the little boy who made me a mom, so fragile, fighting every day to be with us. You can never plan your future, so don't!!

After my birthday, Ryan really declined, and on 6 July, I had Dr Billi come to check on him. Of course, when she was here, he seemed "ok".

We had so many visitors that day, and I got up to leave the room. Ryan shouted, "Mommy!". That was the last thing he said. He even sat up that day and gave kisses to my Mom and sister.

My Dad had also come down to visit us, the grandparents and friends. Our house was like a train station.

Duncan and Amy came for dinner, and we had just sat down for burgers when Ryan started having another seizure. We tried to control it and phoned Deon, but nothing was helping, so we had to take him to the hospital. We just left our house full of visitors and raced through to the hospital.

Deon met us there, and we were admitted straight away.

12

Chapter 12

Our Warrior is Tired

Lauren

Our phones did not stop, so we decided to create a group where we could update everyone at the same time, as repeating everything was becoming very emotional.

Deon tried all sorts of medicines, but we could not control the seizures.

We both slept at the hospital that night, and my mom stayed with Matthew and James at our house. The next day, Michelle Meiring (the palliative care nurse) came, and we fitted Ryan with a syringe driver, which meant he would be getting medicine continuously.

We agreed that once he was stable, we would be discharged, and Ryan could go home.

We wanted him to die at home around people who loved him, but unfortunately, we never got him stable enough.

The next three days blended into each other as we were so overwhelmed by what was happening. Luckily, we were given a private room in the paediatric ward, which was quite separate from the rest of the ward, and Deon told us to make ourselves at home.

Visitors came all through the day and night, and Paul and I stayed at the hospital 24/7.

I am amazed at how different people react to traumatic situations. You get the ones who are there for you every minute, making sandwiches and bringing you meals, and then you get the ones who ask you when the funeral will be as they are planning a holiday; seriously, my child hasn't even died yet!!

Matthew and James were brought to the hospital, too, and we were so happy to see them as we hadn't seen them in a few days.

Matthew scooted around the ward on his little black bike as though he owned the place, but not knowing what was happening, and when we saw James, we realised he had gotten his front teeth; with everything going on, we hadn't noticed.

Paul

I loved Matti's innocence and almost ignorance of everything around him; he was content and happy in himself. While Ryan would often pick up on situations, Matti did not; he just lived in a very happy place, enjoying his life. It was really wonderful to watch, and it often left me in awe. Perhaps that is how life should be, no worries - "Hakuna Matata"

Lauren

Visitors came and went all through the day. My brother was away at the time, so my Dad organised for him to come back early, and as soon as he landed, he came to the hospital. A friend bumped into us at the hospital, not knowing we were there, so we popped in to see Ryan. When I walked her out, I told her that Ryan was not going to make it home this time, and she was so shocked and just cried.

By Saturday, Ryan was in a coma, and every time I had to send a message saying he was in a coma, the predictive text would say he was in China, and I remember thinking, *fuck, I wish he was in China.* The seizures did not stop for one second, and it was really distressing seeing him like that. Paul broke down and asked if there was anything else we could do. Every day after the visitors left, we would sit with Ryan and tell him he could go, we would be okay, and he could go, but he just kept fighting.

On the Monday, the room was full of people, and I remember Deon walking in and saying, "Wow, you really did make yourselves at home." We all had pizza and drinks, and everyone looked like they were staying for the night.

My mom had one of the best pizzas that night. I can still remember the butternut, rocket, onion, and pumpkin seeds clearly.

Paul

It was all quite surreal; we all knew the inevitable, but I guess pretended it wasn't there, and for that time, we had enjoyed the company of our close friends and family. We gained a lot of solace through that and really got to appreciate true friendship.

Lauren

Deon walked over to Ryan, and the buzzing room suddenly went quiet.

He told us part of Ryan's brain had shut down, and slowly, the rest would, too. He drew a picture for everyone to see what he meant, and it was hard to hear but good, as I think until that point, some friends and family still hoped Ryan would pull through. After Deon left, there was an awkward silence. No one knew what to do, including Paul and I.

I was on the bed with Ryan, and Paul was on the other side of the room. I sent him a message and asked him what he wanted to do. Should we tell people to stay or go? We agreed everyone should say goodbye and leave so we could be alone with Ryan.

So, at about 10:30 p.m., everyone slowly started to leave. I can't imagine how they must have been feeling, knowing they probably wouldn't see Ryan again.

When everyone left, we quietly got into bed with our boy in between us, told him we loved him, and told him again that he could go.

Paul

I almost pleaded with him. It was really tough.

Lauren

Deon had mentioned that sometimes dying people get something called the death rattle, and I remember thinking I really hope Ryan doesn't, but we didn't know what to expect. We decided we didn't want any monitors on him, just the syringe with the seizure medicine. We fell asleep, and in the night, I remember waking up and hearing that his breathing had changed. It wasn't scary. It was just different.

At 5:30 a.m., I woke up with a jolt as if someone had given me a fright. I looked over at my boy, and I knew he was gone. I checked and double-checked, but he wasn't breathing anymore. He just lay there peacefully, still warm and still beautiful!

I woke Paul up and told him that Ryan had gone. What a horrible way to be woken up. He burst into tears, and we held each other tightly. The nightmare of Ryan's suffering was over.

Paul

Tears of incredibly deep sadness, but of relief for him, fear of how our life would be changed without him, flooding memories of his life and what he meant to us. I was also cross; it seemed so unfair, everything he had to go through for 9 years, so short yet so long.

Lauren

After what seemed to be ages of holding each other and crying, I buzzed for the nurse, and when she came in and saw Ryan, she hugged us. It was one of the nurses we knew well.

We asked her to phone Deon, and I switched off the machine and held my boy.

My boy was gone. The nightmare of seizures had ended; he had fought so hard for so long, and now he was at peace. Ryan Peter Spagnoletti passed away on 10 July 2014, aged 9. Paul was going to phone his parents and some friends, so I went downstairs with my cigarettes, my go-to habit under stress, and phoned my mom first and then my dad and the tears came; saying it out loud, reality hit me. My son had just died. He actually died. Years of thinking it wasn't going to happen to us just blew up in my face.

Our friend Duncan was the first to arrive; he got to the room door and just stood there. Paul and I got up robot-like, and we all hugged. He told us it took him a few minutes to get into the hospital. He physically had to force himself up the stairs.

He was broken for us. Ryan was his godchild. He and Amy had been with us every step of Ryan's journey and, over the last few days, had been at the hospital every day.

Paul

This was a huge moment. Duncan is, without question, the guy that rocks up in a crisis. He is that guy; when there is a wolf at the door, he doesn't hide inside. He runs out to meet it. To explain this, he developed a security app at a point in time that did many things but relied on the community responding and coming out of their homes to protect others. I had often asked, but would people? I know you would, but would most not hide in their homes and protect their own? I would do that for sure. But even though he, as he said, took some time to come in the door, he did, and that I will never forget, always cherish and hugely respect. Would I do the same? I would hope so!

People often lack words as to what to say in the face of loss, but I can honestly say you don't have to say or do anything. Just rock up. That in itself means more than any words, food baskets, letters, emails, or texts. Just rock up ... I remember this from Ryan's funeral. I was so disappointed to hear people had made an effort to come and then had not waited for me to see them and give them the respect they deserved for rocking up. I guess, though, and to be fair, nobody knows what to say, and just coming is a big thing. Actually, facing people can be super difficult.

Lauren

Deon arrived, and we all hugged again. It didn't feel real, and yet our boy lay lifeless on the bed. We chatted to Deon about what the next steps were, and he said he would phone the funeral home when we were ready and warned us that when they did come, it would be very hard, and maybe we didn't want to be in the room, but we both decided that we wanted to.

The nurse came in and gave Ryan a little wash, and afterwards, I thought I should have done that, but in the situation, we didn't know what we should be doing.

We waited for the family to come, and Duncan and Amy went to get coffee for everyone. Every time someone new arrived, the tears would start up again. They would go in and see Ryan, and after a while, when we felt ready, we chatted to Deon, and he phoned the funeral home.

When they arrived, everyone said their goodbyes and left the room. Paul and I stayed in the room, and our parents stood at the door.

They came in with a trolley and carefully put Ryan on it. It was too much. Paul ended up punching the wall. I just stood there, watching. After they had put him on, they covered him in plastic; I lost it, I couldn't breathe, I started hyperventilating, and I just couldn't be in there any longer. I ran out of the room; my heart felt like it was going to jump out of my chest, and my chest was burning. I ran to the exit and felt like I was screaming at the nurse to open the door so I could get out. The poor nurse was in such a state she was fumbling with the code, but eventually, I could get out. My Mom ran after me, and I just broke down in the hallway. I felt claustrophobic, like someone had hit me in my chest. I was pretty much close to hysterical. A few minutes later, the trolley came past with my baby on it, all covered in a blanket, and I just sat there crying uncontrollably. Paul came out to find me, and we just cried together. Our "big boy" was gone.

Paul

I guess the reality and gravity of the situation finally hit home and hard. Hitting the wall was an attempt to blow off steam and vent my huge anger at what had just transpired. It is fascinating how often men show frustration physically. I often wonder why I did that, and it doesn't make any sense. It didn't make me feel any better. Watching them put Ryan in that plastic was the most awful thing I have ever had to witness in my life. Only a few hours ago, we begged Tiger to stop fighting and let go. Now, a few hours later, I would do anything to have him back, even as sick as he was. It was a haunting moment!

Lauren

Our parents left, and we slowly went back into the room and gathered our stuff. Ryan was gone. He was actually gone. After years of thinking it would be different, how it would never happen to us, it just did.

We drove home in silence, lost in our thoughts and exhausted from the last few days. Within a few minutes of being home, our house was buzzing with visitors. Matthew and James had slept at Paul's parents' the previous night and arrived soon after we got home. I felt so sad for them. They had just lost their big brother but didn't know it. I gave them both the biggest hugs. Our phones did not stop, and I just didn't have the capacity to answer all the calls. Messages came from all over the world, and then came the flowers.

Every few hours, a new arrangement of flowers and meals to feed a small kingdom arrived.

That day and the next was a flurry of visitors, and in between, some family and friends helped me organise the funeral.

The day after Ryan passed away, we had to go to the funeral home to chat with them. We decided we wanted Ryan cremated, so we chose a simple coffin. I also didn't want the coffin in the church. They asked us if we wanted to see him again, but we didn't want to. It was hard enough in the hospital a few minutes after he had passed away. His body had already started changing then, so I didn't want to see my boy now. I had the perfect picture of him in my head, and I didn't want that picture to be changed.

My family has a printing shop, and they very kindly helped with the church service program. My mom organised announcements in the paper for us. The support we received was unbelievable. I knew I had to get the funeral out of the way as I was feeling very anxious about it, so we decided to have it three days later. I phoned my doctor and asked for medication for the day as I felt I couldn't physically get myself to the church. We told everyone to wear bright colours, and we had colourful little paper butterflies made for everyone to wear.

The day before the funeral, Shelly and I went and had tattoos done. I added a butterfly and a J for James to my boys' initials, and Shelly had an R and a butterfly done.

So what do you wear to your son's funeral??

You tell everyone to wear bright colours so we can celebrate Ryan's life, but you really feel like wearing black pyjamas.

In the end, I decided to wear a bit of both. Purple pants and a black top I had bought years before I even had my boys. It had a beautiful silver lace butterfly on the back.

The day of the funeral arrived, and I woke up and felt strangely calm. I knew my boy was pain-free, and that is what I was going to focus on. I went outside for my morning cigarette, and there on the step was an orange butterfly. I put my finger out, and it climbed on. I asked, "Ryan, is that you?" and obviously got no reply. It stayed on my finger the whole time, but eventually, I had to go get ready, so I carefully put it on the boy's horse tyre swing called Beauty, and do you know, that butterfly stayed there for a whole week and then disappeared. And that wasn't the only butterfly encounter we had. A butterfly landed on Paul's mom's shoulder during Matthew's horse riding lesson the week after and stayed there for nearly half the lesson. Another butterfly was sitting on Shelly's car windscreen one day a few weeks after that. I knew my boy was ok.

We decided Matthew and James shouldn't come to the funeral, so we organised a babysitter for them. They were so young, and we selfishly thought it would be better for us if they weren't there.

Family from Johannesburg arrived that morning and came straight to our house, and then we all left for the church together. When we arrived at the church, we went into the office and met the minister before the service started. It was our parents, siblings, and us, and we said a little prayer. Then, we walked into the church from the front. The church was packed; every seat was taken, and there were people sitting where the choir normally sits and people standing in the back. Our little boy had touched so many lives. Our friends, family, school teachers, doctors and nurses were all there to celebrate our big boy's life.

Paul

I think, in many ways, the sight of so many people paying tribute to our boy really brought about an additional calmness and almost gratefulness that his life had not been in vain. As Lauren has said, Tiger had really touched so many people's lives in so many ways, and in his short 9 years of life, probably in more ways than many of us will in a full lifetime. His story still does and is a constant reminder of never taking small things for granted, embracing what you can, and laughing through it all.

I loved the idea of celebrating, not mourning his life. I wore a bright orange jacket, the brightest thing I could find in my cupboard. Like many times in my life, I strangely felt extremely calm, relaxed and at ease throughout the ceremony. In fact, I can remember smiling and thanking people at the tea afterwards, not with a smile of bravery but genuine gratefulness that 1, people had come and 2, that Ryan had made such an impact. This is going to sound weird based on the circumstances, but I was genuinely overcome with pride for what my little boy had achieved. A boy who could not eat, talk, walk, and had limited hearing and vision filled (overflowed) a church full of people. Quite incredible.

Lauren

The service was beautiful; the minister had kept it short, but it was lovely.

Paul and Duncan spoke, and my cousin's husband read a poem, which I wanted. There was a big screen behind the minister where a collage of beautiful memories was played, and as long as I didn't look at that, I was going to be fine.

After the service, we left the church, followed by family and had tea in the church hall, where everyone paid their respects to us, which I was so grateful for, but also found quite draining to keep thanking everyone. I just stood there greeting and hugging everyone very politely like an emotionless robot.

Obviously, certain people really triggered me, like when I hugged Deon and his staff and my nanny. Some people cried when they hugged me, and I just couldn't handle that, so they got a quick hug and then had to move on quickly. Once all the hugging was over, I felt much better, and it felt like a weight had been lifted off my shoulders. I had survived my son's funeral. We had organised 100 balloons for after the tea and were going to go to the beach, so close friends and family were invited to join us for that.

We went home, got Matthew and James, and met everyone on Hout Bay beach. It was a typical winter day. The sky was very dark, the rain threatened to come, and the wind was pumping!!

Everyone grabbed a balloon, and we had little note cards that you could write a message on and then stick to your balloon if you wanted to. Once everyone was ready, we gathered in a circle and on the count of three, we all let our balloons go. They went off wildly, dancing in the wind, and we all stood there watching them disappear in the distance.

It was so fitting for our boy, who loved life so fiercely.

We all returned to our house, where the family very kindly made soups and bread. It was a long day, but Ryan would have loved it, all his favourite people together, celebrating him. And he deserved to be celebrated, Ryan Peter Spagnoletti, the little boy with the biggest personality and a love for people and life.

I think I slept well that night, and when I woke up the next day, I thought, *'Is Ryan really gone?'*

13

Chapter 13

First Year Without Ryan

Lauren

The next few weeks blurred together; we carried on as usual, but nothing was usual.

It was interesting seeing people you knew after Ryan passed away; they either ran the other way, just didn't say anything at all or had the most stupid comments, trying to make us feel better but actually making the situation worse.

My worst was meeting new people; the first question they ask is, "How many children do you have?" We didn't know what to say.

Do you lie, say two, and deny you had Ryan, or say three but one passed away, and then watch the person run or stand awkwardly? I started calling it conversation suicide and have so many stories of when this happened.

After months of being housebound because Ryan couldn't leave our bed, all of a sudden, we could go out. It was so weird.

We went away with our very good friends, as we often did, and although it felt like something was missing, it was also nice to have a little bit of freedom just to get away. To escape our new reality, even if only for a few days.

I struggled at night to get back into my "old" sleeping position because, for months, I slept on the edge of the bed so Ryan could sleep between us. Ryan always had his little arm tucked around my neck, and I found myself putting my own arm around my neck at night.

I took some time off work, but not a lot. I felt I needed to be busy and have some kind of routine.

As for food, my goodness, I didn't cook for about three months after Ryan died. We had so many meals, and someone had set up a meal roster, so we got dinner every night. It was amazing not to have to worry about food.

We spent a lot of quality time with the boys and just really enjoyed being parents to James, our healthy, happy, no-fuss baby. This little boy arrived during such a traumatic time, and unfortunately, the focus was not on him, so it was nice to really get to know James.

I think poor little Matthew was very confused with what was happening but loved spending time with James, playing with him on the floor, bathing with him and trying to steal his dummy.

Of course, there was always this "thing" in the back of our heads that we were going to have to go through this again with Matthew, but we tried to focus on the present and not get too worried about the future; we still had plenty time anyway, Matthew was only 6 years old and " healthier" than Ryan so we still had at least another four years until we had to deal with that again, so we put it at the back of our minds.

The medical conference was happening in September this year, and I had already told them I wasn't coming as Ryan was so sick, but after Ryan passed away, I felt such a strong need to go. Paul was not in the same space as me, so I convinced my mom to come with me.

Paul

I couldn't think of anything worse than going to the CS conference that year. The thought that that song at the end of the conference would be about my boy was not an idea I was loving. For Lauren, I knew it would bring her "peace" to be surrounded by people who understood and appreciated what we had been through. She drew strength from that type of thing, and I completely got that. Many people that we interacted with had no idea how to deal with the conversation, whereas many of the people at the conference had lost one or more children or were facing the reality of losing their child.

I needed to move on, and going "backwards" was not an option; the conference to me was this: dwelling on something I couldn't change. I needed to focus on what I could influence/change. That meant my 2 boys, Lauren, friends, work, and sport. I decided, with difficulty, as I knew Lauren needed me there, not to go to the conference, and Lauren's mom would go. Naturally, if Lauren's mom didn't go, I would've gone, so I was relieved that she was open to the trip.

Lauren

The planning and admin for the conference started, this time we only had about 6 weeks to organise everything, plus we needed to get James a passport.

I messaged Susie, and she was more than happy for us to use her flat again.

My mom had never been to the UK, so there was quite a bit of excitement, although I also felt very anxious. I would have to take the lead in getting around. Normally, Paul did that. There was also the actual retreat to worry about; I felt I could not support my mom the way she supported me. We dealt with things differently, and I felt I did not have the capacity to hold her up if needed.

The packing was interesting. If I thought we had loads of luggage before, boy oh boy, was I mistaken.

James needed so much stuff. He was dairy intolerant, so I wanted to take everything with me; all his meals, milk, and babies needed lots of extra clothes.

The amount of luggage was ridiculous, and I didn't know how we would get from one place to the other with all our bags and a double pram.

The day arrived, and there was no turning back.

We should have known the trip would be challenging when Matthew had an upset tummy before we boarded the plane, and things did not improve. We were in a row of four, but James didn't get his own seat as he was under 1, so unfortunately, some poor soul got to be at the end of our row.

The flight was disastrous; Matthew's tummy didn't improve, and we basically changed nappies the whole flight. The pump went off, there was vomiting, and my mom and I got leaky nappies on our pants. It was a long flight, but luckily, the boys did get some sleep.

I remember trying to sleep and then getting an uneasy feeling, and I opened my eyes to find the guy next to me standing up and just staring at me!!

We landed, and I thought, thank god that was over.

Paul's brother picked us up from the airport, and we barely got all the bags in his station wagon. We stunk, and I would hate to know what he thought.

We arrived at his house, and Paul's parents were there as they were visiting. We gave the boys to them, had a much-needed shower, and felt like new people.

We had brunch and spent the morning with them, which was lovely, but we decided it was time to try and head to our hotel.

Adam dropped us at the train station, but because it was a Sunday, not all the trains were running, and the ones that were couldn't take us directly to where we wanted to go. I started to feel completely stressed about how we were going to manage all our luggage and find our way. Nevertheless, it had to be done, so we said goodbye and off we went.

Two trains later, we were walking to Susie's flat. Thank goodness I remembered how to get there.

We stopped at the little convenience shop on the way and bought two microwave meals for dinner. It had been a long day, so we weren't going to attempt to go out for dinner or hassle with making our own.

It was going to be an early night for all of us so we could be fresh for the next day of exploring.

We decided to take the red bus first; that way, we could see most of the big sightseeing attractions, and then we could always go back and spend more time with the ones we wanted. We bought a day pass, and off we went.

James had now picked up Matthew's bug, so it was fun and games. Thankfully, we were the only passengers at the bottom of the bus because James had a massive vomit all over the seat and the floor and, luckily, not on us. We wiped up as much as we could and changed James into clean clothes.

We decided to get off at the palace and try to see the changing of the guards. What a mistake, every tourist was there at the same time so we couldn't see anything.

We then walked to St James Park and had a little picnic, and I still remember the boys crawling after each other and having so much fun. I have the cutest photos of them.

We got on the bus again and went to Madame Tussaud's. The boys were not too interested, but every now and then, I would make them pose with either my mom or me for a photo. We "saw" George Clooney, Nelson Mandela, Valentino Rossi, and Christina Aguilera. I have a photo of me holding James, and I'm smiling for the photo, and James has his hands all over Christina's breasts!!

While we were there, I got a message to say that Taylor-Louise had just passed away; I just sat down on the floor and cried. I was completely heartbroken. I had spent a lot of time with Jayde and Taylor-Louise. Taylor-Louise and Matthew were very similar; we always joked they were boyfriend and girlfriend.

We left there and eventually found another bus. I really wasn't in the mood to do any more sightseeing, but it was London, and we were there for so short a time, so we needed to make the best of it.

We set off for Trafalgar Square. Our moods had definitely changed, and I was getting quite irritated with just about everything. It had been a long day out.

We arrived at Trafalgar Square and walked around for a bit but then decided it was actually time to head back. The problem was the buses had now stopped running. It was late, so we walked and walked for what felt like forever and then when we couldn't walk anymore, we caught a taxi back to the hotel. Another early night was needed.

My mom woke up the next day with a tummy bug, so we took a bit longer to leave the house.

She really wasn't feeling great, what a holiday! The day's plan was to go to the London Eye and do some shopping. We got to the London Eye easily enough. I was getting to know my way around, and the queue was crazy long, but we really wanted to go up, so we had no other choice but to queue.

Then, what do you know, was our luck changing? We were put in a much shorter queue; I'm not sure if it was because we had a pram or disabled children, but who cared? We were in the express queue. Our turn came, and off we went, and no, our luck had not changed. Matthew made a huge poo while we were up there. For those of you who haven't been, the London Eye is a smallish capsule with quite a few people in it, so a stinky nappy in a confined space was not ideal, but what could we do? We just made the most of it and took lots of pics, trying to ignore the smell.

As soon as we landed back on earth, we quickly headed off to the changing room, and then it was time to shop. My poor mom was not feeling a hundred per cent.

We hit Oxford Street next and had a blast shopping and looking at all the shops; we bought a few things from Primark for the boys and ourselves. Despite our terrible exchange rate, it still worked out well-priced. We went into Swarovski to look at some jewellery. I was carrying James, and Matthew was in the pram laden with bags and jackets. Next, Matthew stood up in the pram, and the whole pram toppled to one side; luckily, Matthew was fine, but we got the most deathly stares, so we quickly gathered our things and left. On the way back to the flat, we decided to stop at Harrods as it was close to the flat.

Our London time had come to an end, and the next day, we were catching the train to Manchester, which was not going to be a walk in the park. We woke up early and made our way to the Euston train station. The station was huge, and coming from South Africa, we were not used to using public transport.

We found the train, and it was a huge rush to find decent seats and enough space for all our luggage, but we made it, and we could now relax as someone was fetching us from the station and taking us straight to the conference. The train trip was great. We ate some snacks and took in the scenery. Luckily, all the vomiting and diarrhoea had stopped, and everyone was feeling much better.

We arrived at Manchester train station, and there stood someone with our names on a placard. Let's hope he came in a mini bus!!

In the car on the way there, I felt a real sense of going home but then also some anxiety as this would be my first retreat without Ryan. I think my mom felt equally anxious as this would be her first time meeting other CS children, and she had no idea what to expect from the retreat. There were going to be lots of new families this year I hadn't met but had had some contact with.

We walked in and received the same friendly welcome I remembered receiving two years before. Only a few of the international families were there, as the retreat only officially started the next day. I saw Jayne, and I could feel my big smile changing to such emotion as we hugged so tightly.

The last time I saw her, I had two 'healthy' CS children. Now, I had one CS child, a dead child and a healthy child.

I saw Amy and the rest of the Hughes family, and like always, Matthew was king-ding-a-ling and was off with someone, only to be seen later when I had to go find him.

James stayed with us as he was at that age when he was quite aware of strangers. By staying with us, I mean we chased after a crawling 9-month-old. I spent a lot of time with the people I knew, Cath, Jayne and Gill.

As always, it was heartbreaking to see which children hadn't made it this year and just as sad seeing the children who had made it and how they had aged.

I met some lovely new families from the US. I met Knox and his mom, Scarlett; Julianne and her mom, Christina; Aaron from the US; a little boy from Japan; Jess and her mum Jo, from the UK; Cameron from the UK; Hussan from the UK; Julie from Germany; Geoffrey from France; and Kenny from France; and some of the children I had met before were also there.

Josie, Nick, Tom and Terri. I totally fell in love with Hussan. He was the size of a four-month-old but was 3 years old. I held him for ages and knew in my heart he wouldn't live much longer. It seemed with CS, the smaller you were, the younger you died.

I also loved Cameron; he used to ride his little scooter all over the show; he was much bigger than the boys but still took a dummy. He reminded me so much of Ryan, so I had a very soft spot for him.

Terri looked good and was still walking around and talking. My mom fell in love with little Knox. He was also very little, so he spent a lot of time in people's arms.

Josie was well and had brought her doll baby.

Amy and Nick were always together, and often Nick would sit on Amy's lap in the wheelchair, and someone would push them around.

Jess reminded me a lot of Matthew, and they were similar in size. The two of them seemed to quite like each other. Julianne was just so sweet and played so nicely with James and a balloon, crawling after each other. And, of course, little Tom, seeing him, I felt so sad. He looked and reminded me so much of Ryan.

I wonder if he wondered where Ryan was. I spent a lot of time with Tom, maybe trying to be closer to "Ryan", who knows? One day, I was taking photos of everyone, and Tom came up to me and started taking a photo of me taking a photo of him, it is one of my favourite photos. He then took photos of us with his camera, and his little finger was over the lens, so his fingertip was in every photo.

That afternoon, we had talks with the doctor, which I remembered to be a really inspiring, hope-giving experience. We were really lucky to have doctors all over the world committed to CS, and I remember the first talk we went to; we were in awe of these doctors trying to find a cure, and we really felt hopeful after the talk, but this talk was different, I was different.

Two years before, I had 2 relatively healthy CS children. Now, I had just lost my oldest baby.

I felt myself sitting there, and I could feel the anger boiling in me, not with the doctors, not with anyone in particular, just angry because I knew there would never be a cure, and as I looked over at the new parents, I saw the same look I had the first time I had heard the doctors talk. I felt terribly sad for them- if only they knew.

Jayde arrived that afternoon, which was very brave of her. We got on really well, and Taylor and Matthew were very similar. We always spent a lot of time together at the retreats because we both smoked so that we would keep each other company outside.

I went to say hi to her, and immediately we connected, two Moms grieving their babies.

Every year at the conference, there is a remembrance tree, and they play Leona Lewis' *Run*, a terribly sad song, before our party night kicks off. Up until now, those two things have been beautiful but very sad for me, but this year is going to be so much worse. Ryan's photo was going to be on the tree, and when the song plays, Ryan's photo will be held up.

I felt quite panicked about the whole thing, and when I saw the tree and all the new faces on it, it took my breath away. There was Ryan, my boy, on the tree, a very hard reality pill to swallow. The party night was always loads of fun, so I focused on that, and we all got ready for the evening. There was a knot in my stomach, and I kind of left my mom with James so that I could do what I needed to do. I debated hiding until the song ended but knew I would be well-supported inside. The song came on, and I was with Cath, holding the photo of Ryan, and the tears just flowed for everyone. There is never a dry eye in sight when that song plays. In fact, if I hear it on the radio, I quickly switch it off or change stations.

After the song, I checked on my mom to see if she was okay. She had been standing with other moms, and I knew she had been crying. Once the song was played, I felt like I could enjoy the rest of the evening.

The music started blaring, and the dance floor slowly filled up.

Some people had decided not to join the party, but the majority were there. It really was a fun evening where parents, doctors, CS children, and siblings could enjoy themselves. I took turns dancing with some of the CS children and really had such a special evening. At about 10 p.m., my Mom suggested she take the boys to bed. Probably not the worst idea, as James was only 9 months but I didn't offer to take them. I wanted to soak up every second with my CS family, and it was just something I had to do.

Afterwards, I felt a bit bad that my mom had to go to the room with the boys as she probably also needed this.

Jayde and I went out to the front of the hotel for a smoke and started talking about what we had been through. It was a very emotional conversation; we finished our cigarettes and put them out in the ashtray when it suddenly exploded. We looked at each other in total amazement and said that was a sign from our butterfly children. We stood there a bit gobsmacked when some drunk man was thrown out of the hotel. He came out swearing at everyone and started walking towards a car; Jayde asked him where he thought he was going and told him he couldn't drive. Jayde totally lost her temper and started shouting at this guy. We decided it really was time to go inside now. I think I got to bed after 12 and was knackered. It had been a very long, emotional day.

The next day was the last day at the retreat. We were up early and headed to the local zoo.

We went down for breakfast, and in walked Jayde with a bandaged hand. Oh my gosh, what happened? After I went to bed, she went back outside to check on the guy and helped him into his taxi when he grabbed her, and that's when she punched him!

We all headed out of the hotel into the parking lot, where the buses were waiting for us. We made sure to be on the same bus as Catherine and Richard. The zoo was lovely, and the boys really enjoyed being outside and seeing all the different animals.

We went to the little souvenir shop, and my mom bought the boys each a plastic animal and Thomas a plastic crocodile.

He absolutely loved the crocodile, and on the way back on the bus, he was scaring everyone; I can still hear him calling, in his most precious voice, "Cath, Cath," his mom, trying to get her to turn around so he could scare her.

We arrived back at the hotel and had some tea and cake, and then it was time to say goodbye. I hate goodbyes, especially when you aren't sure if you will see the CS children again.

We said our goodbyes and tried to all be brave by saying 'see you soon'.

After a short while, nearly everyone had left, and only a handful of us were going to stay on but move to a hotel in Wirral.

We were picked up and taken to our hotel, settled in our room, and the plan was to meet for an early dinner.

We met at the restaurant downstairs, so it was nice and convenient. It turned out to be quite a big group, but I had only met most of them during this trip, so I spent much of dinner talking to Jayne.

Madelaine was writing an article on CS. She had asked me before we even met if she could interview me, so after dinner, we met downstairs in the rain, found some shelter, and did the interview. I was very happy to help in any way.

The next day, we went through to another town by train and spent the day wandering around, looking at all the shops and just taking in the scenery. That night, we had dinner again as a big group, as it was our last night before heading home.

Saying goodbye to Jayne and her family was difficult, but I knew I would do everything possible to return the next year.

We were fetched very early the next morning and had a full day of travelling ahead of us.

It had been a really rough trip to start, but I was so glad I had come.

Thankfully, the flight home was non-eventful, and Paul was waiting for us when we arrived. It was good to be home!

Paul

Holy smokes, it was good to have the family home. I had been doing a lot of travelling for work, but this was the longest we had been apart, and to be truthful, I had some guilt for not going, so to see everyone coming from the plane was super exciting. I can still remember James and Matti sitting on the front of the trolley, coming through those airport doors. The joy of seeing my family coming home literally brought tears to my eyes. They were home! :-)

14

Chapter 14

Bittersweet Celebrations And a Much-Needed Break From Reality.

Lauren

It felt like we had just come back from the retreat, and it was time to plan James's first birthday. How could it be our miracle baby was going to be one?

The days leading up to it were very emotional for me. I kept thinking back and remembering how sick Ryan was when James arrived, but here we were with a beautiful, perfectly healthy son. He truly was our miracle baby and when he started walking and talking we were even more in love with him, he showed us what it was like raising a healthy little child and we loved it just as much as raising our special needs boys.

We had a lovely family celebration, and Paul's dad made James the train cake. of course, James was beyond spoilt.

I was just recovering from the party when it was time to plan Christmas, something I absolutely love, but it wasn't quite the same. I was so torn, wanting to be excited, especially for James, and yet it was our first Christmas without Ryan. How were we supposed to be feeling?

Two days after Christmas, Paul and I had booked to go skiing with the family. After our year, it would be a welcome holiday.

It did feel strange leaving the boys, but I knew they would be fine, and also knew Paul and I needed a break from reality, even if it was just for a few days.

The ski trip was amazing and just what we needed. New Year's Eve was strange, though; here we were heading into a new year after a very heartbreaking year, and yet we were doing so without our Ryan. We were on the slopes at 12 a.m. when the fireworks went off. Standing in the snow with our snow jackets, boots, and beanies was stunning, and we toasted to our Ryan.

Paul

If I had to choose my favourite sport it wouldn't be easy, as you may have noticed, I do and have done quite a bit of it. I really enjoy adrenaline-based sports most of all. My mates and family know this. As an example, for my 40th birthday, my mates got me a parachuting experience. It was awesome, and I thoroughly loved it. So, to say alpine skiing was at the top of the list was no surprise, really. Any time I can work out how to get a ski holiday in, I am over the moon, as again, coming from South Africa, this is not an easy or everyday adventure.

It was also going to be amazing to get some time away from everything and spend some epic time with Joss, Sylvia, and their family, as well as some family friends of theirs that we also got along super well with. Everything was lined up for it to be an epic trip.

Lauren, to be honest, is not the biggest fan of skiing, so it is certainly not her ideal holiday, but it is always different to what we are used to. As Sylvia wasn't the biggest skiing fan either, they would have some great quality time together. We had an incredible time in Meribel, made even more famous by Michael Schumacher's unfortunate accident. Although it did not get off to a great start with Sylvia having an accident at the door where we bought our ski passes, which resulted in her badly damaging her ankle and pretty much not being able to ski. It was a really wonderful holiday and one that, for many reasons, will stay in our memories for a long, long time. Special times with special memories and so many laughs it would be hard to count. New Year's at a ski resort is also just so incredible. I found myself once again in a bubble surrounded by snow and fun, escapism at its finest. Joss and I would revisit Meribel a few years later in a very different way, experience-wise, but that is a story for another time; just to say it was a very special time Joss and I shared, just the two of us gliding in the ski lift into and over Meribel recounting a magical holiday a few years earlier, another special experience for different reasons but made all the more special due to the times we had on this New Year's ski holiday.

After a fantastic 10 days, it was time to go home, and whilst we had an incredible time, we were missing the boys terribly, so it was a well-timed holiday, and we looked forward to landing back in our beloved Cape Town, despite there being no snow there.

15

Chapter 15

Our Family Of Four

Lauren

2013 was a strange year for us; we were now a family of four, and although it was easier in some ways, my heart ached for my boy.

For more than a year of having a bedridden child, we could all of a sudden go out whenever we wanted to; it was very strange.

2013, for us, was all about living each day and appreciating every moment.

We had a busy start to the year when Matthew was admitted for a chest infection in March, a month later for itchy skin, which actually resulted in us finding out he had hypertension but not as badly as Ryan. The next month, we were back again and started on medication. By June, everything seemed to have settled.

We went on walks and took the boys to the parks so they could ride their bikes. We went to the beach very early in the morning so Matthew wouldn't get burnt. We did outings with the boys to the aquarium and the zoo and spent lots of time in our pool.

We went to visit my Dad and spent Easter there, the first Easter that James could walk, and it was the most amazing day, watching him run off with his bucket looking for Easter eggs.

Paul

This might seem trivial, but for us, this is our 3rd child, and it was the first time we were able to witness our child really enjoying and experiencing Easter, and it brought tears of joy to our eyes. We were so blessed, and as Lauren has said, the ability to have more freedom now was really epic!

Lauren

The boys spent a lot of time together, even though Matthew was at school every day until lunchtime. I would fetch him while James slept, and as soon as James was awake, the two of them were off, chasing each other on their bikes or Matthew crawling after James.

They swam together, ate together, and bathed together.

The bond between them was amazing; James would help feed Matthew, fetch Matthew's dummy, bike, or toy, look after his big brother, and love him so much. Watching the two of them was heartwarming.

Paul

We have some great pics of the two boys standing next to the bath together. As much as Matti wasn't as "sporty" as Ryan had been, he still loved balls, and James and Matti had loads of fun throwing a rugby ball to each other and chasing things. I even bought Matti a remote-controlled and battery-operated car to zoom around in, which I thought would be great fun for him, but he never really took to it.

Lauren

Although I felt our lives were as normal as they could be after losing a child, I felt people didn't understand what I was going through, so unconsciously, I became less social with some people. I knew I had to go to the medical retreat this year so I could see my CS family. I managed to convince Paul to come with me, so now it was just a matter of the dreaded visas.

The day finally arrived, and I was so excited, although there was also sadness.

I was now going to be one of the moms with a dead child.

The flight was long, but the boys were so good. They managed to sleep nicely, which meant Paul and I got some sleep too.

Paul

As you would have noticed through reading this book, getting some sleep was great, but there is always a little drama. It seems when it comes to our boys, this flight was no different.

After snoozing for a while, I decided to get up to go to the bathroom. In standing up, I accidentally stepped on Matti's feeding tube, resulting in it being pulled out from his stomach! You might remember earlier in the book, we spoke of Ryan pulling his out and thinking he was quite clever. That wasn't the only time, and we had to put tubes in many times, so that was no issue. The challenge, we soon learnt, was that the syringe we needed to deflate and reinflate the mickey was in our suitcase down below, not in our hand luggage or Lauren's handbag. It is important to note at this point and to demonstrate how amazing the human body is that this is now an open hole in our child's body, so naturally, the body's instinct is to close it (heal it) to prevent infection, etc. We knew at this point we had 30-45 minutes to get the mickey back in, or we would have to do the op again, this time in London, England, as opposed to Cape Town, South Africa, and during this time, he could not eat or drink! The gravitas of the situation was real.

Despite this, I thought, no problem. The plane would have a medical kit. I was about to learn a lot of things about planes and air protocol that I never knew existed before this moment!

I found an air hostess, calmly explained the situation to her, and told her I needed a syringe. Her expression was of shock. She explained she doubted they would have the necessary syringe in the medical kit but would speak to her supervisor. I also explained the urgency of the situation, and she kindly reacted quickly. It was like being in a game show waiting to see what was in the box; the supervisor opened the box, ... we all waited to see if there was something there. Lauren was in her seat with James and Matti. I now had 3 air hostesses and the supervisor with me. Was it there .... no!! Now what??? The supervisor explained there were 3 medical kits, each requiring a different level of authority to open, so off kit number 2, and a conversation with the head of plane staff, which until then, I didn't know existed. After much consultation and debate, he agreed to open the 2nd kit; we opened it with bated breath, time not on our side and the tension intensifying ... nothing, well at least not the right syringe; it had one bit with a flat head, not the nose which we needed to insert into the mickey.

So now what? To the 3rd, I said, and this is when things got real. I was informed that we had to chat with the pilot, and he had to get permission from a surgeon in the States. A long discussion took place between the head of staff and the pilot. I was trying desperately to get a word into the pilot but was not allowed to. The pilot eventually agreed to call the medical emergency but was also informed that they needed to land the plane under these circumstances! I thought, I just need a syringe, no needle, just the syringe. We don't need to land the plane! Then things got more complicated; the pilot was informed that we were flying over hostile territory in West Africa, and landing was unsafe ... this was just getting ridiculous.

Finally, we got hold of the demarcated surgeon; I thought, finally, I could speak to someone who would understand. By this stage, Lauren was starting to panic a bit and was walking up and down between me and the boys; people were starting to become aware that something was going on, and it was all getting a bit hectic. I was asked to please sit down, and I would be called once there was a plan (that was the polite version!).

I spoke to the surgeon, expecting a nice, understanding guy to be on the other side, but it was anything but that. He didn't understand the whole feeding tube thing and was not comfortable with me performing this, asking me if I had ever done this at altitude. I explained the situation and the challenge I had with the hole closing and him not being able to eat or drink, but we were not getting anywhere. We argued for what seemed like ages. I even told them I would sign a waiver, so all risk was on me, not the airline, as this is what it had become about. They said that wouldn't help, and they would still be liable. To this day, I am not sure how, but somehow, I finally managed to convince them not to land the plane and to open the 3rd medical box. We opened it ...and ....

there was a syringe, thank God. I rushed to Lauren, who had by now inserted the headphone jack into his stomach to keep the hole open (not hygienic, but clever woman!) We brought Matti to where we could lie him down and tried to insert the mickey back into his stomach, but it would not go in; the hole had closed too much. We had to make this work, I thought! The mickey is made of a silicon-type material, so it bends. I thought I needed to make it rigid, so I got an earbud from Lauren, broke it and inserted it into the tube to make it rigid (it felt like a bit of a MacGyver at this point - for those who can remember the TV series). I then asked 2 air hostesses to hold him, sat on top and forced Mickey back in. He screamed (now everyone on the plane was awake). I felt a pop, and it was in ... holy FUCK, what a relief ... we had done it. I think everyone involved was exhausted emotionally. I am not sure if many of the air hostesses ever experienced something like that again. I was just relieved it had worked out ... I now needed to sleep. I was super amazed at my calmness through it all and Lauren's ingenuity with the headphone jack ... what a team we had become ... What a story!

Landing at Heathrow was a relief, to say the least!

Lauren

We flew into Heathrow and decided just to pay the millions and get a taxi directly to Susie's flat.

We unpacked, showered, and then decided to go into London; our time was so short, we wanted to make the most of it. We walked down Oxford Street, looking at all the shops and going into the ones that didn't look too fancy. We took the pram, but James enjoyed walking down the streets and watching all the cars, especially the big red buses.

It was so lovely being in London again and simply walking the streets. The weather was cool but perfect for Matthew.

After a few hours of being outside, it was time to head back and have an early night.

The next day, we went through early to Windsor. Paul and I wanted to take the boys to Legoland. I'm pretty sure I was more excited. Two trains later, we finally arrived in Windsor. We excitedly headed to the kiosk to buy our tickets, only to be told that it was Monday and that Legoland was closed. I was gutted; we had travelled so far, only to be told at the destination that it was closed. We were going to Adam and Judy for early dinner but now had the day free, so we decided to do the red bus tour of Windsor and have lunch, and then we would head to Adam and Judy.

The tour was lovely and chilled, and the boys seemed to really enjoy being on the top with the wind in their hair. Windsor was beautiful, and we at least got to drive past Legoland.

After the tour, we had some lunch, posed for the necessary photos, and off to the train station we went.

It took us two trains to get there, and it felt a bit déjà vu'ish going, but luckily, this time, we didn't have three hundred bags to transport, either.

We had a delicious dinner at their house. Judy had made a salmon dish and vegetables, which was much healthier and tastier than the McDonald's we had for lunch. After dinner, we swapped some presents for the kids, and Matthew and James got identical monkey backpacks.

They were too cute, and then we all headed out for a walk. It was so lovely seeing James bond with his cousins, especially Aaron. They were a year apart and only saw each other once a year, so they didn't know each other, but for most of the walk, they walked hand-in-hand.

It was getting quite late by the time we returned, so I quickly bathed the boys and put them in their pjs. Then it was cousin photo time on the couch, a quick modelling shoot, and we had to say our goodbyes.

Back on the train to the flat, it felt like all we did was catch bloody trains in this place! It had been a very busy day, and everyone was feeling very tired by the time we got back. The next day, we caught a taxi to Euston station, where we would catch a train to Manchester.

Euston station was huge and so busy; I imagined it was like Grand Central station in New York, only because I had never been there.

There were people everywhere, walking in different directions quickly, all wearing black and all looking down at the floor.

When the train schedule board was updated, you would see a flurry of people running to wherever they needed to be, so of course, when our turn came, we scuttled off as quickly as possible to the "line" we needed to be first in the queue as we needed loads of space for all our luggage, plus we all wanted to sit next to each other. Of course, it wasn't easy getting two boys, a double pram and all our bags on to begin with, so needed lots of time to sort ourselves out.

Once on, we could relax. I had brought snacks for us, and we managed to get two seats facing each other with a table in the middle, so it was perfect.

The trip was lovely. We got to see the English countryside. The boys enjoyed looking out the window, too, and occasionally, we would spot a cow or a person.

We arrived in Manchester, and I must admit I had very mixed feelings. I felt a bit anxious but excited, too. I could see Paul did not have mixed feelings at all; it was very clear he had come with me to support me, not to interact with the other parents, and definitely not the other children. His plan was to spend all his time with James, which was absolutely fine with me.

We spotted our driver and made our way over to the car.

It was about a 45-minute drive and pretty quiet in the car.

I just stared out the window, thinking about our trip so far and what was about to come.

Who would be there; what would the children look like; would they still look well, or would they look sickly?

Of course, I was excited about seeing my CS family, the family I knew, but did I have the strength and capacity to meet new moms and their babies?

We arrived at the hotel, gathered our things and headed in; as always, walking in felt like being "home" with the *Amy and Friends* banner and table of goodies at the front door and a friendly face to welcome you. They were lucky that way; they always had new volunteers helping them; some lasted years and others only a short time. Every year, the UK retreat was held at the same place, which was nice in a way, as we all felt very at home and comfortable, but when you've travelled so far, it would also have been nice to explore different places.

We signed in, got our room key, and went to our room. En route, we bumped into Jayne and their family, and there were hugs all around. Not many people had arrived yet, so we went upstairs to unpack our bags and freshen up. The first day of the retreat is always so chilled, and it's lovely to sit and watch all the families arrive.

Some familiar faces and some new overwhelmed faces.

Each year, the retreat seemed to grow so much, which was great in a way that families were finding the support they needed, but it was also sad to think there were more babies diagnosed with Cockayne Syndrome.

There were quite a few families from the US this time. Nick, of course, little Knox, whom I had met the year before, Julianne and Jack, Julie from Germany, and Puk from the Netherlands. And then from the UK, Josie, Katherine, Jess, and my little friend Tom, and a new one, Danny.

The first night is always lovely because it is kind of like a meet and greet, but you can also keep to yourself too if you like.

I found that now that I was a mom with a living CS child and a dead CS child, I felt very torn as to where I belonged at the retreat. I wasn't interested in meeting new moms but could really provide guidance and support to them if I wanted, so I found myself sitting with my familiar friends and every now and then would try and chat with someone new, which took a big effort. I felt I was like a part of the original group; we had an almost duty, but not in a bad way, to welcome the newbies.

The second day is always action-packed, starting with breakfast and then loads of activities for the kids, including sensory play, reptiles, face painting, magicians, an arts and crafts table, ball ponds, and lots more. Paul was entertaining James, and Matthew was, as always, being passed around like king-ding-a-ling and loving every minute of it. After lunch, we did a balloon release, which is always quite emotional, and then we moved on to doctor's talks.

I decided I wasn't going to go; just thinking about it made me angry, so best I stay away.

After the talks, we all got ready for the party night. The theme this year was a onesie party, and Jayne had very kindly bought me a onesie as it was summer in South Africa, so onesies were nowhere to be found. She had bought me a Sully outfit from Monsters Inc.. It was brilliant.

Matthew had his little blue onesie on, which had been Ryan's, and James had a monkey onesie on, and you guessed it, Paul was not participating in the dress-up.

After dinner, we all moved into the big dance room, and the music and lights started.

Then came the dreaded time for the song. Paul left the room with James, and I stayed with Matthew. Thomas held the photo of Ryan.

I looked around the room. Every year, the Hughes children are beyond emotional during the song, and I think, gosh, it must be so hard for them. Families come to their families for support, and they get to meet all the CS children, spend time with them, and love them, but then they also lose them. They are so young and have had so many losses.

My heart really broke for them.

After lots of hugging and checking on everyone, the party resumed, and Paul and James joined in again.

There was lots of dancing and singing, and it felt good to be there.

At about ten, I helped Paul get both boys upstairs and into bed. It had been a long day for them, and they needed to get some sleep. Paul was more than happy to leave the party early.

Once they seemed settled, I went back downstairs to join the party; some families had gone to bed, but the majority were still there.

I danced and chatted until after 12; finally, it was time to go to bed. I was exhausted. It had been a very emotional day, but going to bed meant I only had the next morning with my family, and I always dreaded saying goodbye. The next morning, we woke up, went down for breakfast, and sat in the lounge area, talking to our friends. The last day was always a strange one, as you never knew if you would be coming back the next year. You always hoped you would, but you really didn't know. You also didn't know if your child or their child would be there the next year, either.

We were all called outside and had a group photo of all of us in our red *Amy and Friends* t-shirts. Families slowly started leaving, and we had to start saying our goodbyes as we were flying home that day. We said goodbye to everyone, leaving the Hughes and Laurie families for last. Big hugs and kisses for everyone and a photo of us and the Laurie family, and we were finally ready to go.

Our taxi came, and the airport trip was even quieter than on the way in.

It had been a good trip; my heart felt happy but sad.

Paul

Like Lauren had said, and I had mentioned leading up to this trip, it was not my ideal holiday, but knowing Lauren needed me as well it meant I would spend some quality time with the boys, and that was all I needed to make the best of it. We got to do some cool things. What is always great is neither Lauren nor I are ones for sitting around, especially on holidays. We love exploring and getting the most out of a place, immersing ourselves in the culture of a country, city or town and trying to see as much as it has to offer. This typically makes few of our trips relaxing, and we need a holiday from a holiday on most adventures, but it does make them exciting, and we really get to see loads of things and experience the vibe and soul of places we visit. This trip was no different, and as much as Legoland was a disappointment, touring Windsor, which we wouldn't have had time to do if we had gone to the theme park, was awesome and a great experience, as was the train trip out to Manchester.

The actual conference was certainly not as bad for me as it sounds. It was good to chat with the other dads, and like the first time, nothing directly was ever said, but it is what is not said and a deep understanding we are all in the same boat as men dealing with surreal circumstances that brought solace and a kind of peace. It was also wonderful to spend such a great time with James especially. With the demands of work and day-to-day family life, it was a special time for me to really bond with my youngest son.

Despite what it would appear, it wasn't easy to leave Lauren to do many things on her own, as I knew the emotional baggage it had; I wanted to support her but also knew she needed her space and to surround herself with mom's that truly understood her pain, anxiety and day-to-day challenges a mom in these circumstances faces. These are priceless opportunities. My job was to be there when the music died down and no one else was around. In truth, whilst I was never the one to suggest a trip to the retreat, nor did I get very excited about one that was planned, they were always good. I always, in my own quiet way, was extremely humbled by the experience and also got a great deal of my therapy from knowing that we were not alone on this journey; there were others. They really cared… the *Amy & Friends* family was something super special, and Jayne and Mark, together with their sons, are remarkable people with hearts the size of football fields. Having experienced their warmth and welcome is a real privilege and a testament to the experiences you get from the most unlikely events in life.

This was to be my last trip to the retreat, and I am grateful for the wonderful lessons and the amazing people I met. A part of me, Lauren, would never believe this, would want to go back and chat more with the dads and let them know I was there too, and we got through it and, in many ways, were better for it. I guess the thing stopping me is that I don't really like to go back. I enjoy reflecting, but my nature is to move forward, and forward I must go!

I have a passion and skill for public speaking, so I see myself speaking at events in the future, as I believe there is a great story to share, and it would be a tragedy if I could not help others in similar situations.

Nevertheless, more about that later; it seems I have gone a little off-point :)

Don't you also find it interesting how perception in life is such a real thing? I always share with teams I work with that it is a perception you need to get rid of because perception is in someone's head, and you can't manage it. My goal at the retreat was to support Lauren and be there for her, but to give her space ... in her mind. I didn't want to be there. Fascinating, isn't it? The reality is that in life and in marriage, these are the things we need to manage and ensure don't evolve into crazy thoughts that become a reality. In my opinion, conversation, debate, and openness are the keys to success. We are all different and experience and react to situations differently, and that is cool... it is just important the other party knows why.

Time to head back to sunny SA; I was looking forward to going home.

16

Chapter 16

No Dramas

Lauren

Once home, life quickly got back into its normal routine. Matthew continued to go to Bel Porto and loved it, and James was at my school. We still had our nanny, and in the afternoons, after the boys slept, she would take them for a walk or down to the park. I tried to have some time off in the afternoons, but it is difficult to run your own business from home.

At this stage, I did, however, start seeing someone to help me process Ryan's death. In the first few sessions, I just chatted and cried, and after a session, I felt extremely drained physically and emotionally. After a few sessions, she started giving me little projects to work on; the first one was on Ryan and what he brought to our family. Once I had done that, the next project was on Matthew. Being a middle child, I always had this guilt thing with Matthew: had we done enough for him? After doing "my project" on him, I realised we had actually spared him so much and actually done him a favour by not putting him through as much as Ryan had been through. I am eternally grateful for doing these projects; they really helped me as a Mom realise that we had done enough for Matthew. And who knows, maybe that journaling led us to start this book.

The boys spent lots of time together. I have the most amazing photos of them playing peek-a-boo, swinging, swimming, bathing, sitting on the couch arm-in-arm with their dummies, and watching TV together.

They loved each other so much. Matthew had a better second half of the year with no more hospital admissions, which was great as being admitted was very emotional. Going back to the hospital was hard, very hard. The staff were all amazing, but I found myself repeating events every time we were there.

A second Christmas came without Ryan, and we focused on Matthew and James and the joy Christmas brought them. Of course, we had Matthew's birthday to celebrate, too. It is always tricky trying to decide what to do for Matthew's birthday as he obviously can't do everything, and we also need to be careful about being outside in the sun. Still, this year, we decided to have quite a big party with friends at a children's entertainment park.

We paid for everyone's admission and then bought everyone an ice cream. The kids had so much fun, and it was perfect for Matthew. He went on the little boats, flying horses, real horses, and jungle gyms and swings. It was such a brilliant day out.

New Year came, and all we wanted was a boring, no-drama 2014.

Paul

The relationship between Matti and James was really special, as Lauren mentioned, with lovely memories of them throwing the rugby ball to each other, not in a way most would be visualizing it, but very much like 2 toddlers would, but each time Matti would screech with delight. James would laugh, and their bathtimes were also very special. We have a great picture of them standing next to the bath, showing their naked bums and watching the water fill their bath.

I don't think Lauren could have organised a more appropriate party for Matti, one where friends with kids that we invited to play and be entertained and Matti was in his element as he could do many of the things, even horse ride, which we know was an extremely special and important part of both his and Ryan's weekly lives. Anytime on a horse was a good time for Matti. He also loved water, as you well know by now, so floating around in the little boats was great fun for him. I did my best not to topple us over. It was a super special birthday indeed, one that I remember like it was yesterday.

We also had a very memorable photo shoot on the beach, which, as a backdrop, has wonderful views of Table Mountain. Lauren, the boys and I all wore white shirts and blue jeans, which was great fun. Matti particularly enjoyed it as we were on the beach, and despite it being windy, he had a blast (excuse the pun!)

In November, I had to go to the US for a business trip, coming home with a quick stop over in France where we watched the Boks play the French in a rugby test; what an amazing experience, but as much as I was travelling a lot for business, trips were typically only a few days, so being away for 2 weeks was quite tough and not easy on Lauren, looking after the boys and running a business. But as always, she seemed to manage well, and whilst having a break from real life was nice, I couldn't wait to get home to see my boys. It was always a worry that something might happen and the strain that would put on Lauren if Matti ended up in the hospital. Fortunately, he had a better few months.

17

Chapter 17

The Start Of The End

Lauren

The first year after losing Ryan felt very surreal, and I remember almost just floating along; days mingled into each other. After the first year, you have some sort of normality and routine going. So when the year started, I finally felt I could take a breath as we had started to get used to being a family of four and the "freedom" of not having a sick child in bed.

But that feeling didn't last long. One morning in February, Matthew started vomiting blood, so we raced off to the hospital for a gut biopsy and found chronic ulcers in his oesophagus. He was put on medication, and we stayed the night. It was suggested we change his Mickey, so we went to Vincent Pallotti Hospital that month to do that.

In February, my dear little Tom passed away; the last few days of his life were terrible for me, being so far away. My stomach felt like it had a huge ulcer, and I generally felt completely helpless, not being able to do anything but knowing what my special friends were going through. I was standing in the kitchen when I got the message, and all the emotions of losing a child came flooding back. My heart broke for Cath, Richard and Ellie. Thomas Laurie, you will never be forgotten.

March was quiet, thank goodness, and we decided to do a family holiday in April, which we were really looking forward to.

We drove up to Oudtshoorn, which is about a 5-hour drive and stayed at a place called Buffelsdrift Game Lodge. It was our first time there, so we were very excited about it. Our accommodation was luxury tents, and it overlooked a big watering hole. It was stunning and just what we needed after the year had started. We went on our first game drive, and the boys loved being in the open vehicle and seeing all the animals. That night, we went for dinner, and James wasn't that keen to eat, which is very unusual for him, but we thought maybe he'd had just too much fresh air, so we enjoyed our meal, but just as we were finishing, James vomited all over the floor, so our evening was cut short, and we made our way back to the tent. He had obviously caught a bug and had a few loose stools, but by the next day was a lot better. Our second day there was spent on another game drive in the morning, and then we went to the Cango Wildlife Ranch, which the boys really enjoyed. There was so much to see and do. There were swings and slides and loads of different animals to see. It was such a great day out.

The next day, we went to see the elephants. James thought they were amazing because they played soccer and kicked the ball, but when it was our turn to feed the elephants, both boys screamed when we went close to them. However, we did manage to get a photo of us sitting with them. After our two brilliant nights there, we left and made our way to my dad in Sedgefield, but on the way there, Matthew started vomiting. We arrived at my dad's with a very stinky Matthew, but after a nice bath, he was as good as new. We stayed the night with my dad, and Matthew's vomiting seemed to be getting better until we tried to feed him via his tube. Then the vomiting started again, so we decreased the amount so he was at least getting something in. The next day, we headed off to Malgas, which was situated on a river. There were big lawns to play on and a trampoline, so James was very happy. Matthew's vomiting had stopped, but now he had a runny tummy; we weren't close to any shops, so I couldn't get any Rehydrate for him but thought, *'I'm sure he will be better by the morning.'* But by the evening, he was very lethargic and still had an upset tummy, so we made the decision to leave the holiday early and head home first thing in the morning. What a holiday!

We drove straight from the holiday to the hospital, where Matthew was admitted for dehydration and later found out they thought he was in renal failure. I messaged our paediatrician, who was away but was going to be back in the next day or two, luckily.

When we were admitted, I noticed Matti's temperature was quite low but didn't think much of it at the time; actually, I can't believe none of the nurses found his low temperature unusual. Thankfully, Matthew turned the corner quickly, and we only spent a few days in hospital.

Paul

Around June, James must have thought that all this focus on Matti needed some competition, so he figured it was his turn for his first real accident. This came about when he and Matti threw the rugby ball, which they loved to do. On this occasion, when he was trying to catch the ball, he fell forward onto the patio edge, splitting his head open … leading to his head having to be glued. The scar is still there today, a memory of some great times with his middle brother! Besides the accident, it was always great to watch how the 2 boys entertained themselves, and despite Matti's limitations, they had a great time together. A moment that stands out is a family outing to the Crocodile farm in Stellenbosch. We have some great pics of the boys holding baby Crocs. Matti thought this was very funny and loved it, with us having a lovely picnic at the dam's edge afterwards and special memories with our precious boys as physical brothers. We have also mentioned that our boys, and in particular Matti, experience an allergic reaction/sensitivity to the sun and heat, as well as Matti's love for the beach… not a great combination. Another wonderful memory of 2014 is a trip to Boulders Beach in Cape Town, infamous for its penguins. Matti loved 2 things about this experience - driving us mad as he crawled out into the baking sun at every given moment/chance and being fascinated by these strange and quirky-looking birds. He and James had great fun.

Lauren

This year, I managed to convince my sister to come with me to the retreat. She had never met another CS child, and we had never done a trip together, so it was going to be a lot of firsts.

We decided we wouldn't take James, he would stay with Paul.

I was super excited about our first trip together and for Shelly to meet other children like Matthew and Ryan. Of course, we both loved shopping!! So, the planning began. We booked tickets, got visas and organised accommodation. We had Googled and planned all we wanted to see and do.

18

Chapter 18

Matthews White Flag

Lauren

The month after the hospital admission, I kept a close eye on Matthew. I took his temperature to see if I could get a normal reading. I was struggling to get readings and mentioned it to the doctors but didn't get much response. Then, after chatting to friends, I decided to try to take his temp internally and got a reading, which was 32 degrees.

A few months later, I noticed Matthews's breathing at night had changed a bit, and in July, we went to see Deon about an ongoing ear infection, and I mentioned again about the temperature and that I was getting a temp of 32 degrees when I used the thermometer up Matthews bottom, poor little guy. All of a sudden, it seemed a concern after I had been mentioning it for over a month. The plan was I would come in every week to check his blood pressure and his temperature. Deon was obviously concerned because he chatted with Karen, who emailed Prof Laugel about it. We were only to find out about the email later.

We got into a monotonous routine of going through to the hospital every week to check on Matthew, but besides that, life carried on, and Matthew continued at school because, despite the low body temp, he was fine.

On Saturday, 30 August, we went in to check temp and blood pressure and did a chest x-ray, which was clear. To our surprise, his temperature was 36, which is normal, so I was feeling much happier. Deon came in to see him, and I asked him if he thought it was safe to fly with Matthew, to which Deon replied there was no medical reason why he could not fly at the moment. What a relief! I was so happy to hear that.

We got home from the hospital and were having friends over for a braai, so I put Matthew on his bike and started preparing things. After I had done what I needed to, I went to check on Matthew, who was very quiet. He was sleeping on his bike, poor little guy, probably exhausted from the hospital appointment, we thought, so we put him into bed for a snooze, but for the rest of the day, he seemed very subdued. He didn't sleep well that night either. He was very moany and restless, so the next day I phoned Dr Billi to see if she could see us. I went straight there, and she examined him and said he sounded a bit chesty but not too bad if it got worse. I let her know, but it was probably his ear causing discomfort.

Sunday, he really wasn't great; he was very tired and restless, so that evening, I put him in bed with us, and he had a great sleep. However, on Monday morning, I was really worried about him. He was moaning a lot and just seemed exhausted. I phoned Deon, who was fully booked, but because Deon knows I am not the kind of mom who wants to see him for the little things, he told me to come through and said he would squeeze us in. We left James at school, and Paul and I went through to the hospital. Paul was going to be going to Joburg that day, so I thought he would come with me.

We went straight up to Deon's room and saw him quite quickly. He looked at Matthew, and I could tell he was worried. He sent us for chest X-rays, and by the time we got back to his room, he had the results. We sat down with Matthew lying quietly in the pram, and Deon looked at us, his face very serious and sad, and said, " I think we are losing Matthew".

Paul

Now, let's put things into perspective here. You will remember Ryan fought like crazy. We had "end-of-life" counselling in September, and he only gave up the battle the following June. Matti was riding his bike on Friday and squeaking away very happily, outside of the eventual snooze on the bike, but prior to that, he was his completely usual self, and here we were on Monday afternoon, being told we were losing him, and he was potentially in cardiac arrest. How can that possibly be? There is no question or doubt they were very different yet very similar, but in my mind, Matti would have a longer life. Here he was at seven, as opposed to Ryan being nine, and we were facing losing him ... simply put, we were not prepared in any way or form for this news, nowhere even close ... had we been worried, yes, but not to this extent!

I could not believe what I was hearing; I kind of gave a nervous laugh and said, "Are you fucking joking? We were here three days ago, and everything was fine." He showed us the x-ray, pointed to the grey areas, and explained that all the grey wasn't supposed to be there. he thought

Matthew was in cardiac arrest, but before we phoned the family, he wanted a cardiologist to come and see Matthew. We left there in shock and went to the familiar paediatric ward.

Lauren

We arrived, saw familiar faces and were ushered into a room. Unfortunately, the cardiologist could only get there a bit later, so we sat silently waiting for him. We put Matthew into the bed, and he didn't seem to be fussed about being there. Deon came in to see us and went to check on Matthew in the bed, and Matthew gave him a high five and a little squeal.

Paul had to go out for a bit, so I waited with Matthew. I picked him up and held him in my arms as if he were a tiny newborn. He was all snuggled in his blanket, and I sat on the couch and just stared at his beautiful little face. A few minutes later, Kath Megaw arrived. Deon had phoned her to come to see me, and now I knew it was serious. Deon was calling in the troops to come and see me. We sat, chatted, and had a very hard conversation about what we would do if Matthew stopped breathing. It was one of the hardest conversations I have ever had.

Paul

Despite the conversations we had with Deon earlier in the day, I was going to be quick. To be honest, I was still convinced Matti would bounce back. Spagnoletti's are fighters; he would fight, so all would be good. No worries about being out for an hour or so. Naturally, by the time I got back, in just over an hour, things had gone completely pear-shaped! I walked in, and in no time at all, we were in Deon's room having a very dire conversation. This was all so sudden and completely surreal!

Lauren

With Ryan, we had a plan of what to do and when. We had evidence and results on paper that showed us his body was shutting down, but we had none of that with Matthew, so even talking about the end of his life made no sense. I couldn't make that kind of decision at that moment, and I needed proof. I needed time to process all the shit that had happened that morning. Kath stayed for a bit, then left, and finally, the cardiologist arrived. It seemed to have taken an eternity for him to get there. He set up, and I could feel the anxiety and stress in the room. We all watched silently as he did his tests on Matthews' heart. I prayed over and over again in my head for it to just be pneumonia. After a little while, he turned to us and said Matthew's heart was fine. I nearly hugged him; I was so relieved.

He packed up and left, and we waited for Deon to come back to chat about the plan, but when he came back into the room, it was like a medical drama movie had just started.

Deon told us that they were struggling to get enough oxygen into Matthew, so he needed to be moved to the ICU, and we should phone the family. Phoning grandparents and telling them their grandson is dying and they need to get to the hospital now is not an easy phone call to make, and yet this was the second time we had to do it.

My mom and Shelly were going to leave work and come straight through; they were also going to let the other family know. Paul's parents were going to get James and then come through. Duncan and Amy were going to go to our house and get clothes for us. Word started to spread slowly, and the messages started, but I just couldn't answer all of them; it was too much.

Phoning my dad was hard as he lived the furthest away. He asked if he should come that day, but it was 5 p.m. by that time, and he lived about 5 hours away, so he planned to leave first thing in the morning.

What a fuck up! This wasn't supposed to happen. Matthew still had time with us and had not travelled the same journey as Ryan. That's what we were prepared for a long, horrible road of suffering and morphine. We weren't ready.

Once the phone calls had been made, the medical drama movie seemed to kick up a gear, and we were moved to the ICU. Initially, we were put in a general-type ward next to an elderly person with absolutely no privacy. Then, I'm not sure how, but they gave us a ward reserved for contagious diseases. I was so thankful; it was quiet and away from everyone else.

Paul

This, I have no doubt, was another little intervention from our incredible paed, Deon. Things seemed to be going from serious to out-of-control minute by minute. It seemed like just a few hours ago, everything was okay, and now here we are in a private ICU "tent."

Lauren

They had put Matthew on oxygen, and I'm not sure when exactly, during all the mayhem, he had become almost unresponsive.

The family started arriving, and we gathered outside the ICU and chatted. We really did know how to take over a place. The family were allowed in a few people at a time, and then Paul's parents arrived. When Paul and I saw James, we both burst into tears. Our little miracle baby was just about to lose his second brother, and he had no idea. He is all we would have left.

We told him we were going to take him to see Matthew, so the three of us went in together. Matthew looked different, with tubes going into his nose, but it also looked like he was sleeping. We could tell James felt very uncomfortable being there and couldn't quite understand what was going on, but we could sense emotions were high, so we asked him to give Matthew a big hug and kiss, which he did as he loved his brother so much. My heart was breaking for him; why must he lose both his brothers?

Paul

These two moments will stay with us forever without question. One, the emotion of seeing James at that time, and then, his experience of seeing his brother was, to put it bluntly, devastating for us as parents.

Lauren

We took him out, and Paul's parents went in to see Matthew; we decided James was going to sleep with them that evening, so when they said goodbye to Matthew, they left.

Karen arrived a little later, and we (Deon, Karen and us) all went to a private room to chat. We needed a plan for the next few hours; Deon needed to know what he must do if we couldn't get more oxygen into Matthew. I repeated my whole conversation again, saying I had no proof this was the end, and yet they were saying there were signs that this was the end. It just all seemed like a bloody nightmare. In the end, we decided we wanted them to resuscitate, but we agreed on no machines.

Karen then left, and Deon told us he couldn't find a c-pap mask small enough for Matthew in the hospital, so he went to the Red Cross Children's Hospital to find one.

By this stage, the family group had grown, and slowly, everyone was having a turn to say goodbye to Matthew. Travis arrived with his girlfriend Cindy, and they went in to see Matthew, and I followed. Cindy was on her phone, and the next thing she did was hold the phone to Matthew's ear. She had phoned my Dad, and he was chatting to Matthew. This so took me aback. What a thoughtful thing to think of in such a traumatic time.

At about nine, everyone started leaving, and Paul and I returned to the room with Matthew. I sat on the end of his bed, staring at him, wondering how this happened.

Deon arrived back with a smaller nasal prong c-pap mask, which they quickly fitted onto Matthew, but his oxygen reading was still not great.

Deon stayed for a bit and then went home; it had been a very long day for him, too.

I sat with Matthew, holding his hand, until about 2:30 a.m. and then decided I would sit on the chair. My head was pounding, my eyes were stinging, and my back was sore from how I had been sitting with Matthew. Paul had fallen asleep on the couch a few hours before. I told the nurse to please wake me if anything changed. It felt like I had just closed my eyes when the nurse woke me up. I checked my watch, and it was just after 3 a.m. I went with her to Matthew and could see his heart was going slower by the second. I ran to wake Paul up, and by the time we got back to the bed, which was literally a few meters away, his heartbeat was at 30; we both stood there counting down his heartbeat and telling him to fight. Then, all of a sudden, it was on 0, and the machine beeped that long beep, just like in the movies. The nurse started CPR and injected what I think was adrenalin, and Matthew gasped for air, and we thought, 'T*hank God he's back*,' but then his heart stopped again while Paul and I stood in a corner in disbelief. It honestly was like watching a movie: the poor nurse started CPR again, and in walked Joyce, one of Matthews' wives' from the hospital. Remember the one I told you about earlier in the book, the one Matthew loved so much? I thought, *'Great, she's coming to help, this poor nurse'*, but boy was I wrong; she came in, didn't seem to notice us standing in the corner and didn't seem distressed at all with what was going on and asked the nurse, the nurse who was trying to bring my son back to life, for a pen, a fucking pen. I could not believe it.

I asked, "Aren't you going to help?" She seemed not to hear me and left. My God, how can someone be so heartless? The poor nurse was struggling and once again gave an injection, and Matthew gasped for air again but then was gone again. Another nurse came in just as that happened. I presume she was the head nurse on duty for the evening, and they called his death. I ran over to the bed and frantically picked Matthew up. All the tubes and wires were all over, so I unplugged what I could, and I just held my baby in my arms, rocking slowly while the tears gushed out.

A few minutes later, Deon arrived, and I couldn't even meet his eye; I just sat there rocking Matthew.

My head was still pounding, the tears had relieved some of the sting from my eyes, and my chest was so tight I could barely breathe.

We chatted with Deon and, unfortunately, knew the procedure going forward and this time, we were better prepared for what happened. We would tell Deon when we were ready to phone the funeral home, but first, we had to phone family. I went downstairs to have a cigarette. Yip, I had started smoking again when Matthew was admitted the day before. I phoned my mom first, who said she would come down straight away, and then I phoned my dad, whom I felt desperately sorry for. When I told him, I could hear the massive sadness that he hadn't made it down in time.

I went back upstairs, and Paul had phoned his parents, who couldn't come to the hospital as they had James, and he had phoned Duncan, who was on his way already. I had decided I wanted to wash Matthew before they took him away, so the nurse arranged some clean water and towels. I pulled the curtain around his bed so it was just him and me and wiped his little body clean. I find it so scary that one minute, you have a heartbeat and a warm body, and within minutes of you dying, your body is cold and starts changing colour. I took photos of his little hand where we both had a mole in exactly the same place and a photo of his chubby little feet.

I wiped his face and spiked his hair, and he looked beautiful.

Duncan was the first to arrive, and we sat together, chatting and drinking leftover coke from the night before. The lovely head of the ICU came in. She had just started her shift, and before she had gone to the desk to check what happened in the night, she came to check on Matthew; we presumed she knew, and when she saw him, her face fell, and I realised that she hadn't been told yet, shame, her eyes swelled and she said I'm sorry for your loss, I had no idea.

My mom and Shelly arrived next and went in to see Matthew. When they were done, we told Deon we were ready, and my mom, Shelly and Duncan left the ICU so we could be alone. Our experience with the funeral home and Ryan was very traumatic, but I had decided I was staying until the very end, and I wanted to lay Matthew on the trolley.

The funeral home arrived and laid a blanket on the trolley, and I picked Matthew up and carried him towards the trolley. I bashed his legs on the door going out of the room as I had forgotten they were so stiff, so I gently made my way out of the door, lay him with care on the blanket, and gave him a big kiss on his forehead and covered him with the blanket. They wheeled him away as Deon, Paul, and I hugged each other and cried. What a journey the three of us had been on, and just like that, our CS journey came to an abrupt end.

19

Chapter 19

Our Gentle Soul Send-Off

Paul

The day had been long, at least in particular; the evening had been even longer. The conversation about what we needed to do if Matti was not responding was tough, but in the tough moments, I seemed yet again to have clarity of thought and a strange calmness about things. While it was a hard decision, especially with little warning of such a conversation, it seemed we had the right plan. Perhaps not being able to prepare was a good thing in a way.

The way our precious little angel Matti passed on, with no fuss and no fight, was almost poetic, as it had been his life - chilled, quiet (apart from the beautiful squeaky noises of delight he made), and innocent. I was dumbstruck and devastated. Yes, things had gone completely upside down, and it was more serious than ever before. We had the discussion around life support, but surely he would fight, and we would be talking about how Matti, like his brother before him, had stared death in the face and defied it. No, not our little Matti. I could almost see him going, "Yeah, this is not for me. I am out. I have had a good life. Thanks for the good times and memories, guys ... ciao". I won't lie. I was super cross with Matti. I could not understand why he would not fight, and I distinctly remember saying that to his peaceful little body on the bed. I literally collapsed to the floor and cried for what seemed like hours. I felt broken; wait, I was completely and utterly broken.

There were times in his life when I truly believed he had the potential to rise against the odds and at least walk. He perhaps wasn't as street-wise as Ryan in many ways, but he didn't have the tension in his muscles that restricted his movements quite as much, so I secretly allowed myself to believe that it could be possible. Perhaps as he saw James develop, he would try and succeed, but I guess we (I) would never know, and truthfully, were these his ambitions or mine —absolutely mine. He was a happy, content little boy, trapped in his own world surrounded by love and affection, and as much as he received, he gave back in heaps and bounds. Our little lover, my squeaky little mouse, was gone and all so fast .... WTF!

Lauren

We left the hospital and made our way home, all in silence, in the same clothes we had arrived in the day before. I had a splitting headache, and my body felt like it had been hit by a train.

Our parents would come over, and we would have to let friends and family know and once again plan the funeral. It felt like we had just planned Ryan's.

We also still had to tell James, who was now nearly three.

He arrived with Paul's parents, and I felt such sadness for him; this little boy who two years ago had two brothers now had none. He was old enough to understand that Matthew was missing but too young to comprehend death. We sat him down and told him that Matthew was in heaven with Ryan. His heart got tired and stopped beating.

Paul

This became quite a challenge for us, that being the explanation of Matti's passing and, to be honest, his life in general. Rightly so, James would ask where his brother was and when he was coming back, but how do you explain death? We as adults can't really comprehend it, can we? We all know that life on Earth is finite, but we don't actually believe it, do we? We live as if there is no end to it all, so how in the world do you explain this to a child of 3 and answer the questions as he gets older and becomes more inquisitive?

Our route and answer were, to be honest, and I think that has been good for James and, for that matter, ourselves. We made the decision from Ryan that the boys (then only Ryan) would remain a part of our lives and our families forever. He would not be forgotten, and we would celebrate him, his life and what he taught us through significant events (birthdays, Xmas, Angelversaries, etc.) and through pictures throughout the house representing great moments of his life. We would do the same with Matti so James would know his brothers, and they would not disappear and fade away as memories. I heard a friend once say (not knowing that I/we heard) that it was like a shrine, and I guess in a way it is, but it is more about celebrating them and not denying what a beautiful and impactful part of their lives they were. Again, people react differently. I guess if one has never quite gone through this, how do you know? But judgment is easy until you are in someone's shoes, isn't it? We are so proud of all 3 of our boys, and we are so blessed to be able to celebrate their lives, be it in the flesh with James or through pictures with Ryan and Matthew. Call it a shrine. I call it **love**, **honour** and **celebration**.

James still finds it difficult to comprehend their passing and not having brothers when he should, as well as understanding their disabilities, but this has provided him with a great deep EQ that many children don't possess. I believe this will stand him in good stead in life. His compassion for people, giving of himself, selflessness, and drive are already amazing traits he has developed, making me so proud to be his dad.

Lauren

The messages, flowers and meals started pouring in the minute we got home, and within a few hours, the house was filled with family and close friends. We decided to have the funeral quickly once again. I didn't want to drag it out, so the funeral was set for three days, hence giving people enough time to get to us. I'm not quite sure how I functioned those first two days. I suppose my body was on autopilot somehow, except when I had to choose photos for the hymn sheet and slide show. I just couldn't do it. Looking at photos was too painful, and I would just break down. Thank goodness for the support of family and friends who helped me plan everything.

We would have the service at the family church, followed by tea, and then close family and friends would go to the beach to do a balloon release and then lunch at our house. déjà vu all over again.

The day after Matthew died, we had to go to the funeral home to finalise things there, and I remember the person's face who worked there. Their eyes were desperately sad for us when they saw us, as we had been there two years before. This time, it was quicker as we knew what we wanted, and like Ryan's funeral, we didn't want the coffin there. They would contact us after the funeral to arrange the collection of the ashes.

The day before the funeral, Shelly and I decided we were going to get another tattoo.

I had ordered a necklace from the States, and a friend was going to bring it to the retreat, so I was due to get it in two weeks, but all of a sudden, the necklace was not good enough. I decided I wanted the saying tattooed. I hadn't decided where, but I knew I wanted it, so off we went.

I told the tattoo artist what I wanted and the kind of font I liked, and he suggested down my arm. My initial thought was, '*Oh my gosh, that's huge*', but the position made perfect sense. I also wanted to add on to my old one, so he started by adding a butterfly to my "m" initial and then started on my other arm, "Some only dream of angels; I held one in my arms". It was beautiful!

When I got home, the priest was at our house. Paul had gone for a cycle, so my mom was with James. I felt a bit strange walking in with bandaged wrists and arms, just having had a tattoo, but he was very interested and wanted to see it. We chatted about the service and how everything was going to proceed, and then he left. My mom and Shelly left soon after Paul arrived home, and being "alone" in the house with no visitors was strange.

Paul

My bike had become a bit of an escape, and there was nothing quite like getting on the road and just feeling the wind across my face, with time to reflect on the days that had passed and really how surreal everything was. One has to come back to reality, though, at some stage. Over the years, I found 3 things that helped me get through the trauma of losing my first two sons: 1) our family and Lauren's strength and courage; naturally, James became a huge focus. 2) work, which had always been a big focus and part of life but was an escape on many dark days, and 3) my sport, be it cycling, running or golf, just being out in the open air with mates allowed me to be in a very happy place. With respect to point 1, without Lauren and especially James, I am not sure we would have gotten through this all quite as well. James was a true blessing, and he enabled us to remain a family unit and have something to focus on and to look forward to in the future … he gave us something to be positive about despite the immense sadness we felt. This we knew, and this is what we focused our energy on.

Lauren

That evening, we both sat and wrote our speeches for the funeral. I surprised myself but knew that I wanted to speak.

I tried to go to bed relatively early as I felt exhausted, and since Matthew had died, I was really struggling to sleep. The next morning, I woke up feeling okay. I forced down some breakfast and had already decided I was going to wear a butterfly top and jeans. It was 5 September, so it had started to warm up a little, but not enough for a summer dress. I showered, got dressed, and spiked my hair with the hair straightener in honour of Matthew; he always had spiky hair.

James was going to stay home, and we would collect him after the church service on the way to the beach. We were going to meet at the church half an hour before with the grandparents and have a chat with the priest. An hour before we were going to leave, the family from Joburg arrived. Although it was lovely seeing them, it really wasn't a happy occasion. Paul's brother had also flown in from London but was going to meet us at the church. It felt like the Joburg family had just arrived, and then we had to leave for the church. We arrived at the church, and I got out of the car, didn't make eye contact with anyone, and went straight into the office to meet the priest. We had a brief chat and prayed. The grandparents went into the church first, and we followed.

This time, I was more prepared and gave everyone strict instructions on where to sit. I sat between Shelly and Paul, and my mom sat beside Shelly. Once again, the church was packed with friends, family, staff from Matthew's school, hospital staff, volunteers from SARDA, families from my school, work colleagues, friends, family, and all our doctors.

We had decided we didn't want a long, drawn-out service, so the priest's speech was short and sweet, but then, when he asked if anyone wanted to say something, to our surprise, there were quite a few people.

Nomsa spoke and told everyone how she told Matthew to help her find a husband, that her prayer had been answered, and that she had found someone. Our friend James spoke, as did Matthew's teacher, Tania. Duncan spoke on behalf of my Mom and Shelly, and Adam spoke, and then it was my turn. I was so nervous but knew deep in my heart I needed to do this. I spoke and barely looked at anyone, and before I knew it, I had done it. Paul was the last person to talk, and then we sang a hymn. The priest closed off, and we left the church first to go to the hall.

Paul

Again, like Ryan's funeral, we asked people to wear bright colours to show a celebration of his life. We were once again staggered at the number of people who arrived at the service; it was extremely humbling to know that your sons, with such short lives, had impacted so many people. The speeches were beautiful and a tribute to Matti's life and what he meant to people.

Lauren

We hugged close family, and before we knew it, there was a long queue waiting to chat with each of us. The queue seemed never to end, and I found it extremely difficult and draining to chat with everyone, but all these people loved Matthew, so it was my duty to chat with all of them.

Eventually, the queue came to an end, and people started leaving. I felt a huge weight fall from my shoulders; the funeral was over. When only close friends and family were left, we decided it was time to get James and head to the beach.

We went to fetch James, and everyone went straight to the beach.

It was a breathless day on the beach. We all huddled in a circle and shouted, "We love you, Matthew," and let go of our balloons. The balloons slowly and peacefully floated up like there was no hurry. It was such a surreal feeling. Two years ago, we had Ryan's funeral and released balloons that flew up with so much energy, and in a whirlwind, they were gone, and here I was again, watching the balloons for Matthew float so peacefully away.

My gentle soul!

Everyone came back to our house for lunch, and I put a book out for people to write down memories, but no one did; everyone was still in as much shock as we were.

By the time everyone left, I felt extremely tired, a combination of not sleeping well and just the emotional drain of the day. Although I couldn't wait to get into bed, there was now a lot of anxiety about going to bed, as that was where Matthews' last few hours haunted me.

Because the family had come down for the funeral, we organised a Sunday lunch. It was a lovely day spent with them, and yet it felt like a huge mountain sat on my shoulders.

My ear was a bit tender the whole day, yet I couldn't see anything. Paul had to travel to Joburg the next day, so the plan was that Shelly would come and stay with me while Paul was away. He was only going for a few days and travelled a lot, so I knew everything would be fine, but the company would probably be a distraction.

But the next day, I woke up with swollen cheeks and glands and knew it was mumps.

I felt terrible; this was the last thing I needed, but I needed to be "okay" for James.

That night, we put James into bed, and I planned to go to bed as soon as I could. I hadn't eaten much, so I felt very low. We were sorting out the kitchen and making something to drink when I heard a strange noise coming from James' room.

It was James, and he couldn't breathe; he was having a croup attack. I temporarily forgot what we had to do in the panic and not feeling well. He was crying and saying he couldn't breathe, and the more he cried, the more he panicked and couldn't breathe. It was horrible. I went to our first aid box, got out all his meds, and phoned Doctor Billi, who thankfully answered and reminded me what to do. Thank goodness Shelly was there. Between the two of us, we tried to calm him down and administer medication. The whole episode probably lasted close to an hour, but it felt like many hours. I really thought we would have to take him to the hospital, which made me want to panic even more. Could I handle going back a few days after losing Matthew? Thank God it didn't come to that, and we got everything under control. I decided I would sleep with James that night so I could monitor his breathing, and thankfully, he didn't have another attack.

My mumps lasted over a week. I was exhausted and couldn't eat properly, and the food tasted different. Once I started feeling better, I tried spending as much time as possible with James.

The sleeping got worse, and I resorted to trying to listen to music with headphones in and even that didn't help. Sleep deprivation is really a killer.

I got into my mission mode, wrote notes and letters to Deon, Dr Billi and the one nurse in the ICU unit and dropped them all off. I inquired about play therapists for James and looked up ways of 'remembering your son' and what books to read to James.

Paul was travelling every week to Joburg now, so I had a lot of time to myself, which unfortunately turned out not to be a good thing. One night, I broke down in tears and told him I felt like I was dealing with everything on my own. He agreed to try not to travel so much.

Paul

This was a huge watershed moment for me. In my mind, Lauren was doing okay, and the travelling wasn't so bad. At the time, I was heading up the sales team for our SAP team at EOH. This was a big role, and as most of our business was in Jhb, I needed to be there, and my leadership team wanted me there. Nothing really prepared me for this call from Lauren, and I can still remember standing outside the EOH office building (block D) having this call. I immediately went upstairs and asked my MD for a meeting, which he agreed to, and told him we needed to make some changes to my travel schedule, which he agreed to. We would naturally phase down my travel, with a plan of creating a Cape Town role for me, which took longer than planned, but we eventually achieved this goal.

20

Chapter 20

First Conference Without Our Boys

Lauren

Shelly and I still hadn't officially decided what we were going to do about our trip. It all seemed too much to try to think about, but time was ticking, and we had to decide.

Eventually, I decided I wanted to go, it was going to be shit hard, and I was going to be forced to deal with emotions that I did not want to deal with, but I felt I had to go.

We had to organise the death certificate so we could send it to the airlines to get reimbursed for Matthews's ticket. People asked if I was going to take James and how James would be if I just disappeared on holiday, and I just couldn't think of taking James with me. I had to do this for myself, and Paul wasn't going to travel that week so he would be with James.

CHAPTER 20

Packing for the trip took me forever. I couldn't seem to concentrate or make any decisions on what to take. Shelly and I had decided we weren't going to plan anything, which is unheard of for me, and we would chat about it on the plane.

Arriving at the airport was hard; there were supposed to be three of us travelling: me, Shelly and Matthew. It was supposed to be this exciting adventure for Shelly and me, and introducing her to my CS family. Instead, I felt overwhelmed and heartsore. The flight over was fine. Our seats were at the back, which was great because we didn't have anyone behind us, but we were right at the toilet and being a light sleeper did not help the situation. Nevertheless, when we arrived at Heathrow, I had to put on my big girl panties and get us to Susi's flat. I had decided we were going to get the subway straight from Heathrow, and it was so easy. I can't believe I hadn't done it before; it took us straight to Knightsbridge.

We arrived a bit early, and they were still cleaning our flat, but that didn't stop us; we hopped into the shower and felt refreshed to hit Oxford Street. We walked for hours and eventually made our way back to the flat to change as we were meeting my cousin for dinner. Back on the tube to meet Darron, which was lovely, then before we knew it, it was time to go again, back on the tube and another walk back to the flat. What a busy first day. That night, we slept well.

The next day we went sightseeing. We did the London Eye and the palace and basically walked around London, then met Shelly's friend for lunch. We were exhausted but headed back to the flat to get ready for our night out to see The Lion King, a present from my brother-in-law.

I was very excited. It's almost a bucket list item that if you go to London or New York, you have to see a show.

We arrived and ordered drinks and the most expensive popcorn I had ever bought.

The show was spectacular; the costumes, the music, and obviously being African, it was extra special. We made our way home and collapsed into the bed. Our time in London was short but extremely busy. Next stop, Manchester.

The next day, we packed up our things and made our way to the train station, where we would catch a train to Manchester, where someone would pick us up and take us to the Retreat.

Public transport really was a hack, and I missed my car.

The train ride was beautiful and very relaxing, although I knew in my heart it would be so difficult seeing everyone at the retreat without either of my boys.

We arrived in Manchester, and our ride was waiting for us.

He loaded our bags, and as soon as we were in the car, he asked us where we were from; our answer was "South Africa", expecting him not to know where it was, "where about?" he asked. "Cape Town," we said. He then told us his wife was South African and promptly phoned her to tell her he was giving South Africans a lift. She started chatting in Afrikaans, and I quickly responded that my Afrikaans was "kak" (slang for rubbish). We were all laughing so much that he dropped his phone down the side of his car seat, and we all shouted goodbye to her as he hung up the phone on his car kit.

Well, that took my mind off everything for a bit!

We arrived at the retreat, and I slowly walked in, Shelly behind me, not knowing what to expect.

As always, there were smiley faces to greet us. I walked around to the lounge area, and there was a room full of familiar faces, all sitting, laughing and chatting. I had only seen some faces on Facebook, but I felt I knew them.

Kathy and Heidi from Canada and America were there, Daniella from Denmark, and Christina and Stephanie from America. After introducing ourselves, I saw Jayne, and my heart just felt sore. We hugged each other for ages, and the tears threatened to come, but I fought them off.

We went to put our bags in our room and then came downstairs again.

Families from all over were arriving, so many new families. :-(I couldn't bring myself to introduce myself to any of the new parents. I watched them arrive with such high hopes and expectations; how could I introduce myself as the Mom of two dead children? So I just sat in the corner watching. I knew I was only going to socialise with my close crew, the moms I had known for years, the moms that knew my boys. I couldn't possibly try to make new friends with people who didn't even know my boys; it would be too hard.

Shelly was very happy to walk around and meet new people, which was great as she had never met another CS child before, and they were all so special.

That evening, Cath, Richard and Ellie arrived; it was such a surreal feeling.

Here we were, none of us with our sons, on our first retreat as the moms whose children had died.

We had already decided to spend all our time together, and if that meant sitting out of the retreat, so be it.

That night, we sat up drinking rum and eating chocolates from all over the world with a select small group of moms. It was lovely seeing them all again. The next day, more families arrived, some I had seen on Facebook and others I had never seen.

We all got stickers, and mine said, "Lauren, Mom, to butterfly Ryan and Matthew." It just didn't seem real. Even when I walked past the tree of remembrance, I was horrified to see Matthew's photo on it, right next to Ryan's and Tom's.

The day was spent chatting with moms I knew, and occasionally, I would take a walk around but couldn't bring myself to chat with many people and holding a CS child was out of the question.

That night, we sat in our little group, and Julianne wanted to come and sit on my lap. At first, it was okay, but then some of her behaviours and sounds started reminding me of Matthew, and I could feel myself start to panic. I slowly reached down into my bag and grabbed my cigarettes. I could physically feel my body go into a panic, and I started hyperventilating. It felt like the room was so tiny, and I needed to escape. I lifted Julianne up, plopped her onto Shelly's lap without warning to anyone, and ran as fast as I could outside.

As soon as I was outside, I took a few big breaths to calm down, lit a cigarette and inhaled deeply. The tears just flowed! And there I found Robin, sitting at the table, drinking his beer and smoking. I could always talk openly with Robin. He was someone who made you feel comfortable, and what I really liked about him was his ability to talk openly about how he felt. Shelly appeared a few minutes later to see how I was, and I apologised for the no warning of Julianne suddenly landing on her lap.

The rest of the evening was quiet. I stuck to myself and didn't mingle; it had been a draining day.

The next day was much the same: I kept to myself mostly and stayed with moms I knew.

Kathy showed us how to weave cut-up clothing through hessian bags; I forget what they were planning to make, but I remember thinking it was a brilliant idea.

I chatted to the doctors and one or two new moms, but that was it. I didn't listen to the doctor's talk as I felt really angry, which was unfair as they were trying to help.

That night was the big "party" night, and this year the theme was superheroes. Shelly and I had decided to wear black dresses and have fairy wings with Ryan and Matthew's photos on them.

Dinner was lovely, but I knew "the song" was coming up and debated whether I wanted to be in the room.

In the end, Cath and I decided we were going to stay together. I had already warned Shelly how sad it was going to be.

I had given Jess one of Matthew's onesies, and she was now wearing it, so I was giving her a cuddle when the song that they had played at Tom's memorial came on. So I got onto a chair, and we were holding up glow sticks and dancing, and the floodgates opened; I couldn't stop crying, and Jess was getting quite heavy, too, so one of the Dads helped me down from the chair and took Jess. I then went to stand with Shelly and Cath as the awfully sad song came on, and everyone in the room swayed sadly, holding up photos of the CS angels. After the song, it is like we all have to check on each other, so you go around crying but making sure everyone is okay.

After gathering ourselves and once the tears had dried up, the dancing music started, and everyone either left, started dancing with the children or went to the bar. So Shell, Cath, Jayde, Robin, and I hit the bar, and we were introduced to a very delicious drink: Malibu and Red Bull. After a few shots, we were ready to hit the dance floor, and I went to get Julianne, apologised to her Mom, and whisked her off to dance. The evening was lovely, and I knew I needed to be there. No one understands me like the other CS moms do.

We stayed up quite late. I wanted to spend as much time as I could with the moms, but eventually, bed called.

The next day, we basically had our group photo and breakfast, and then families started leaving.

Saying goodbye to Jayne, her family, and Cath and Richard was always hard, but even more so this time. Would I come back next year?

Shelly and I said our goodbyes and a taxi drove us to our hotel in Wirral, where we would be spending a day. That evening, we had dinner with all the families that were spending another day, and the next day, we planned to go shopping and to the Liverpool waterfront to try out the rum bar.

Our time there was lovely, and our ride to the airport was spent thinking of the last few days. Emotions were all over the place, and I felt emotionally drained but happy I had come. The flight home was spent talking about our trip, and I knew that when I got home, I would have to face my new reality, my life without Matthew, my life without CS.

But when I arrived and walked through the gate, I was greeted by a running James shouting, "Mommy", and getting a huge hug. My very heavy heart felt a tiny bit lighter.

Paul

I must say it was strange, and I felt a little anxious about Lauren going; it was great that Shelly was there to support her, and it would be great for her too, but I wondered whether I should not be more supportive, yet at the same time, knowing Lauren needed this, and time to herself, with people she trusted, loved and had been "there" would be good for her. In hindsight, I think it was the right decision; what it did provide for me was some amazing bonding time with James and a good reality check on priorities, that being that family needed to be this and not work - not that work wasn't important. Still, certainly, the amount of travelling I was doing was not healthy for our family, especially now. Lauren and James needed a present husband and father, and I guess I also needed to deal with the loss of my second son and not hide behind work. We all know where and how that would end, and it would not have been pretty.

James and I had a great week, and I thoroughly enjoyed it. I was now more determined and in the right frame of mind to change my work structure. Fortunately, I had a very understanding and humane management team and company that understood and, most importantly, supported me and my family. One of my fondest memories was 2 days after Matthew passed away. I received a call from my Group CEO's personal assistant asking if I would take a call from Asher. I was a bit stunned; I wasn't sure he knew who I was. I was reasonably senior in the business but not at the level that I interacted with the group CEO. Nevertheless, I said sure, no problem. Asher went on to pass on his condolences but took the time to understand the boys' backgrounds, challenges and what led to their passing. We must have chatted for 15-20 minutes, something I cherished and certainly appreciated. It spoke highly of the business I was part of.

21

Chapter 21

Life Without CS

Lauren

The next few months were difficult for me. I struggled to sleep and generally was very down. I tried to carry on as normal, but Matthew's death really knocked me. I focused on James and the real blessing that he was, but it was hard as he had questions about the death of his brother and couldn't understand why he was gone.

One day, he wasn't feeling well, and when I asked him what was wrong, he said his heart was stopping; this broke my heart. My poor little boy had been through so much.

Paul was travelling a lot, and one night, I just broke down and told him I felt as though I was dealing with everything myself. I really wasn't coping and needed extra support from him.

We decided to plan a holiday for December, something to look forward to would be good.

So, in December, we flew to Durban and went to a family resort for a few days.

It was our first family trip with only the three of us, and it felt very strange. Firstly, we only had to pack clothes, no medication, no machines and secondly, Durban is very hot and sunny, somewhere we could never have gone with the boys. We spent the mornings on the beach and relaxed by the pool in the afternoon.

I took a photo of James at the beach, jumping in the waves and to this day, it is one of my favourite photos. A healthy boy was running and jumping. In the photo, he is in mid-air, and for me, it symbolises the freedom his brothers never had but now do.

Life without Cockayne Syndrome is so different; it really feels like a chapter in my life that happened so long ago.

For months, I missed the hospital and doctor visits, the medication, that bloody pump, the mickey, the vomiting, the therapies, and all the other shit that came with it. That is all I knew for so long, and within a minute, it all changed. It was all gone. All I had to do now was be a Mom to James.

Every year, we remember our boys. We celebrate their birthdays and remember them at Christmas and on their Angelversaries. They will forever be a part of us, and James is such a wonderful mix of both his brothers. He loves his sport and loves to laugh like Ryan but can be reserved like Matthew.

People ask me how Paul and I got through what we did; honestly, I can't say how. I think because we react differently to things, we complement each other, but saying that, we also respect how the other feels and reacts and how each other needs to process things. We worked as a team and knew the parts to play.

People say we are an inspiration, and I keep asking myself why. Because we went through a lot of shit and came out the other side? For me, there was never another choice; we fought for our boys to the very end. I found a strength in me I never knew I had. The real inspiration was my boys; they lived life despite all their challenges and did it with a smile.

CS stands for courage and strength, two things I learnt from two very little people.

Two very little people who made me a Mom and the person I am today.

Paul

At the end of it all, as Lauren has said, despite the trauma and hard things we dealt with, given the choice to do it all again, I would put my hand up without hesitation. Sure, we would do a few things differently, but the boys gave us the opportunity to see life for what it is, the pure, simplest form of it. We learned to celebrate and appreciate the little things, we learned to support each other, we met some truly amazing people, and we have had a blessed, collectively, 12 years with our boys. The best part is we now get to share that with James, a healthy, loving boy, and as Lauren said, having the best of our precious first 2 boys reflected in James, along with him being able-bodied, what a blessing. I had another tattoo done, this one for James: 2 rings circling my arm representing completeness, and a Chinese sign meaning blessed

….. blessed to have James, blessed to have so many learnings from Ryan and Matti, completeness that we now have James to celebrate life with and completeness that Ryan and Matti showed me humility and acceptance.

Lauren and I are better for it from having our boys; they will always be a part of our lives, family, and memories, and we celebrate through pictures and special events.

There is obviously so much more that we could have written, but we hope we have given you a glimpse of our beautiful boys' lives.

Thank you for reading our story. Our hope is that this will inspire or help people struggling with life challenges to know that you can always get through it and, more importantly, be better for it.

#gonebutneverforgotten

Welcome to Holland

By Emily Perl Kingsley

I am often asked to describe the experience of raising a child with a disability - to try to help people who have not shared that unique experience to understand it, to imagine how it would feel. It's like this......

When you're going to have a baby, it's like planning a fabulous vacation trip - to Italy. You buy a bunch of guidebooks and make your wonderful plans. The Coliseum. The Michelangelo David. The gondolas in Venice. You may learn some handy phrases in Italian. It's all very exciting.

After months of eager anticipation, the day finally arrives. You pack your bags, and off you go. Several hours later, the plane lands. The flight attendant comes in and says, "Welcome to Holland."

"Holland?!?" you say. "What do you mean, Holland?? I signed up for Italy! I'm supposed to be in Italy. All my life, I've dreamed of going to Italy."

But there's been a change in the flight plan. They've landed in Holland, and you must stay there.

The important thing is that they haven't taken you to a horrible, disgusting, filthy place full of pestilence, famine and disease. It's just a different place.

So you must go out and buy new guidebooks. And you must learn a whole new language. And you will meet a whole new group of people you would never have met.

It's just a different place. It's slower-paced than Italy, less flashy than Italy. But after you've been there for a while and you catch your breath, you look around.... and you begin to notice that Holland has windmills....and Holland has tulips. Holland even has Rembrandts.

But everyone you know is busy coming and going from Italy... and they're all bragging about what a wonderful time they had there. And for the rest of your life, you will say, "Yes, that's where I was supposed to go. That's what I had planned."

And the pain of that will never, ever, ever, ever go away... because the loss of that dream is a very, very significant loss.

But... if you spend your life mourning the fact that you didn't get to Italy, you may never be free to enjoy the very special, very lovely things ... about Holland.

22

Conclusion

As for every person, life's journey is filled with joy, sadness, love, heartache, opportunity, reflection and disappointment. Our lives as a family bear testament to all these emotions of the ups and downs of life, in many cases relating to the extremes of what a family can endure. We wanted to share our story with you and not only reflect on these emotions through sharing our journey but, most importantly, show that despite seemingly impossible obstacles and challenges, we got through it and live to benefit from the lessons we gained from facing these situations.

Epilogue

As we draw the final pages of this book to a close, we want to extend our heartfelt gratitude to you for sharing the extraordinary journey of our two brave and beautiful boys. Though tragically short, their lives left an indelible mark on our hearts and our family.

In the years following their passing, we have found strength and resilience we never knew we possessed. We are now involved in various endeavours, such as advocacy for rare genetic syndromes and supporting families facing similar challenges. If you're reading this and going through your own personal trials, please don't hesitate to reach out. We understand your struggle's depth and are here to offer support and hope.

May the story of our sons serve as a testament to the human spirit's capacity to endure and overcome even the most seemingly insurmountable obstacles. In their memory, we strive to spread awareness and inspire others to find the strength within themselves.

Thank you for joining us on this profound journey.

Afterword

Our hope is that this story will provide solace, inspiration, and the knowledge that, no matter how difficult the journey, you can emerge on the other side stronger and filled with hope.

If you find yourself facing adversity, we invite you to reach out. ljspag3@gmail.com

Printed in Great Britain
by Amazon

37983483R00136